KU-064-333

Praise for *Transforming the Mother Wound*

"*Transforming the Mother Wound* is a rich, thoughtful book that holds you safely in its arms along a potent inner journey. It illuminates the enormous transformational potential that lies in healing our relationship with our mothers, and with the Great Mother. This is an essential companion for all those with a sacred contract to serve the Goddess—and for those who recognize that their deepest healing is linked inextricably to their Divine calling."

— **Sophie Bashford**, author of *You Are a Goddess: Working with the Sacred Feminine to Awaken, Heal and Transform*

"In this wise and compassionate guide, Monika Carless takes the reader on a journey through healing the mother wound. Weaving story, ritual, journal, meditation, and other psychospiritual depth perspectives, this book is a healing and empowering exploration that can help you witness the complexities of your own motherline, cultivate self-compassion, and bring you home to yourself."

— **Danielle Blackwood**, author of *The Twelve Faces of the Goddess* and *A Lantern in the Dark*

"*Transforming the Mother Wound* is a gorgeous road map that invites us into right relationship with the first heartbeat we ever hear. Through rituals, ceremonies, and reflections, Monika holds sacred space for us to transform our relationship with the mothering dynamics that inform our lives. This book is a must-read for all who are breaking cycles of the past and planting new seeds for the future generations."

— **Asha Frost**, author of *You Are the Medicine* and *The Sacred Medicine Oracle*

"*Transforming the Mother Wound* is a beautifully written and mystical book by Wise Woman, author, and mentor, Monika Carless. Filled with sacred rituals, teachings of the archetypes, and practical tools to deepen our understanding of mother, Monika helps us rewrite and reframe the story we've created around our primary relationship and the one we have with ourselves. Poetry that speaks to the soul and stunning artwork is woven into each chapter. This is a must-read for women looking to reclaim their power, love themselves deeper, and transform a core or ancestral wound."

— **Dina Strada**, author of *If I'm Honest: A No BS Guide to Loving Yourself, Navigating Relationships, and Trusting the Journey*

"In *Transforming the Mother Wound*, Monika brings us along on a journey of self-exploration, where the wound becomes the wisdom-keeper. There is a sacred pathway to finding peace with what was, what is, and what can be, which is what the practices and rituals in this book explore. This guide is a gentle way to work with inner shadows, bring harmony to the nervous system, and ignite a new relationship with the Mother energy we all innately long for."

— **Shereen Sun**, author of *Radiant Wildheart: A Guide to Awaken Your Inner Artist and Live Your Creative Mission*

"Monika ably reminds us all of the deep, rich, powerful promise of the woman who has rediscovered her voice to heal this hard world of ours."

— **Waylon Lewis**, author of *It's Never too Late to Fall in Love with your Life* and founder of Elephant Journal

Transforming the

Mother
Wound

Published in the United Kingdom by:
Hay House UK Ltd, The Sixth Floor, Watson House,
54 Baker Street, London W1U 7BU
Tel: +44 (0)20 3927 7290; Fax: +44 (0)20 3927 7291; www.hayhouse.co.uk

Published in the United States of America by:
Hay House Inc., PO Box 5100, Carlsbad, CA 92018-5100
Tel: (1) 760 431 7695 or (800) 654 5126
Fax: (1) 760 431 6948 or (800) 650 5115; www.hayhouse.com

Published in Australia by:
Hay House Australia Ltd, 18/36 Ralph St, Alexandria NSW 2015
Tel: (61) 2 9669 4299; Fax: (61) 2 9669 4144; www.hayhouse.com.au

Published in India by:
Hay House Publishers India, Muskaan Complex, Plot No.3, B-2,
Vasant Kunj, New Delhi 110 070
Tel: (91) 11 4176 1620; Fax: (91) 11 4176 1630; www.hayhouse.co.in

Text © Monika Carless, 2024

Cover design: Barbara LeVan Fisher
Interior design: Bryn Starr Best
Interior illustrations: Angie Shea

The moral rights of the author have been asserted.

All rights reserved. No part of this book may be reproduced by any mechanical, photographic or electronic process, or in the form of a phonographic recording; nor may it be stored in a retrieval system, transmitted or otherwise be copied for public or private use, other than for 'fair use' as brief quotations embodied in articles and reviews, without prior written permission of the publisher.

The information given in this book should not be treated as a substitute for professional medical advice; always consult a medical practitioner. Any use of information in this book is at the reader's discretion and risk. Neither the author nor the publisher can be held responsible for any loss, claim or damage arising out of the use, or misuse, of the suggestions made, the failure to take medical advice or for any material on third-party websites.

A catalogue record for this book is available from the British Library.

Tradepaper ISBN: 978-1-83782-196-9
E-book ISBN: 978-1-4019-7689-7
Audiobook ISBN: 978-1-4019-7690-3

This product uses responsibly sourced papers and/or recycled materials. For more information, see www.hayhouse.co.uk.

Printed and bound by CPI Group (UK) Ltd, Croydon CR0 4YY

MIX
Paper | Supporting
responsible forestry
FSC
www.fsc.org   FSC® C171272

Transforming the

Mother Wound

>———•••••••••———<

SACRED PRACTICES FOR
HEALING YOUR INNER
WISE WOMAN THROUGH
RITUAL AND GROUNDED
SPIRITUALITY

>———•••••••••———<

Monika Carless

HAY HOUSE

Carlsbad, California • New York City
London • Sydney • New Delhi

Contents

For my mother Teresa,
who gave me life and purpose
and my mother Henryka,
who awoke me to it.

*"The things that women reclaim
are often their own voice, their own values,
their imagination, their clairvoyance, their stories,
their ancient memories. If we go for the deeper,
and the darker, and the less known,
we will touch the bones."*

— CLARISSA PINKOLA ESTÉS

*"As long as we
resist the pain or the truth—
the heart healing, and therefore the light,
which so many desire to enter—
is blocked.*

*And we stay stuck in things that aren't
our true self, our highest good, sometimes
only to avoid a few moments of 'truth.'*

*Start where you are.
Don't reschedule change.
Move with what's possible."*

— SOPHIE GREGOIRE, FROM "SHE IS THE MOON"

Important Note: Shamanic rituals are indigenous to various cultures, such as the Indo-European Celts, North and South American First Nation Tribes, Indigenous Australians, and Polynesian cultures, to name a few. As a Wise Woman of Eastern European shamanic tradition, I lean toward my own culture but also rely on the wisdom of cultures around the world. When incorporating magic from outside my own heritage, I bow to the teachers, ancestors, and culture, acknowledging their sovereignty and carefully hold their wisdom in my body.

Introduction

Surrendering to the Sacred Womb of Healing

I am so very honored to share with you a map for finding peace with the story of your mother wound. If you are here, your soul has called you to this work.

This is a dynamic exploration focused on transformation at a cellular, intergenerational level with interactive pages that invite you to participate in your healing journey.

Throughout this journey, you may find that your creativity, intuition, soul frequency, and empathy are deepened, along with your connection to yourself, Source, and all life forms.

Embodied and aligned, your body, mind, and spirit will embark on a new path—one of embracing the medicine of past wounds and becoming fearlessly yourself.

The Ancients valued the natural rhythms of the Universe and planet, and in this way, found rootedness in their humanity as well as the sacredness of their infinite natures.

It is in our humanity that we experience all there is: the light, the dark, the inner world, and the outer. All is sacred. You are sacred.

In this work, I undertook to honor the mystery, magic, and unseen elements of transforming core wounds, because life is so much more than what can be quantified through linear science. Life is also your multidimensionality, your humanity, and spirituality. Let us explore together.

*The template for healing the mother wound
is the template we can use for healing all wounds,
because it teaches us to be in harmony
with what is, and with ourselves.*

About Me

My experience with healing the mother wound has been one of the greatest lessons of my life. And writing this book has been my act of devotion to the Consciousness and service to humanity.

I am honored to be part of your rising, Beloved, as others have been part of mine.

The journey of orphanhood, adoption, relocation, challenge, and eventually awakening to my purpose has been an undeniable spiritual initiation. I offer my story, my process, and my gratitude through these pages, created for the collective healing of the mother wound and the Great Mother Herself.

I have always looked for the root of things because that is where the story of anything begins and where it is best understood.

The winding road of healing took me deep into the woods, into something I remembered faintly, until I emerged a witch, a soul-alchemist.

Three long-distance pilgrimages across the wilds of Northern England brought remembrances of past lives, as I connected with ancient memories of the Divine Feminine and my ancestral roots. I expanded into holistic nutrition, organic farming, and local food initiatives. Each step taken, although sometimes seemingly random, came with a deeper understanding of myself, my place in the world, the incredible synchronicity of my life, the wisdom of my wounding, and what I was here to do.

Simultaneously, I grew two free-range daughters, encouraging free thought—unschooling them at times— and always seeking to not repeat the cycle of my turbulent childhood, with well-intentioned but mixed results. They grew, and I grew, realizing in the process that my mother (much like me) had been nursing her own core wounds.

Words and writing became the ultimate medicine for my own mother wound and the portal for this work.

As an initiate of the Munay-Ki Rites, I found direct paths to shedding the skin of core wounds and am honored to pass on these teachings to my community. My life and potent rise from the proverbial ashes of mother wound is now the soil of my teachings.

How to Use This Book

You may find it helpful to skim through the chapters first to see the progression of transformation steps and to familiarize yourself with the path as an intentional integration with the work.

Parts I (Creating Safe Ground) and II (First Steps) are a gentle way to ease yourself in. Our bodies and psyche are very attuned to changes we make in lifestyle—you may notice subtle or unmistakable resonance as you dive in. Sustainable self-healing means that you and your Inner Child feel safe while absorbing these chapters.

Gathering Tools

To anchor your spiritual work in the physical world, I suggest some Wise Woman tools. Part I contains information on journaling, as well as altar creation, which includes tarot cards and any other oracle tools you desire; traditional altar items such as candles, crystals, nature treasures, and representations of Mother or Goddess; photographs from your childhood; and a current photograph of yourself.

Any tools you use or invite into your practice are simply touch points, making it easier to work in both the spiritual and physical realms. Use what you have, or source what you need; either way, make it what you need it to be.

Blessings on your path, Wild, Sovereign One!

*Healing the mother wound
is what the whole village needs.*

PART I

Creating Safe Ground

*We dance with the mother wound to
find our worth and purpose. Our mother may
never actualize into the person we think we need her
to be; and yet, we can become our own center. The fact is,
we have exactly the right mother to launch us
on our wisdom path. She is the portal for our
empowerment. Mother is our awakening.*

A CALL TO CIRCLE

*The mother wound is a portal through
which we walk to awaken unconditional love
and compassion within our hearts. I witness your
courage and your determination for understanding
and healing at such a profound level.*

Imagine that in reading this book, you are joining a circle of sisters at a round table, each of us with equal voice and presence. Women around the world are participating in healing their mother wounds, and you are united through intention. The symbolism of the circle is as infinity itself, a cosmic mystery whose energy holds the codes of everything that is. To sit in the circle is to be part of womb space, to embrace the cyclical nature of life. It is unity and inclusion, wholeness and completion. It is centering.

As part of my dedication and service to you, I cast a magical circle inviting the elements of Air, Water, Earth, Fire, and the Four Directions to your work.

I invite and thank all the spirits and goddesses with whom you resonate. I ask the wisdom of your ancestors to guide you, and call for the temple of your heart to open to what is ahead. May you be embraced by the warmth and safety of this circle.

And so, it is . . .

Queen, Mother, Daughter, Wise Woman,
Lover, Teacher, Maiden, Crone:

The archetypes of the Divine Feminine
express themselves in many ways.

She is not to be contained,
a wildfire that consumes and nourishes, births, and heals.
She is at times a raging river;
other times a silent breeze.

She dances with her guides, ancestors, and angels.
Boundless. Erotic. Wise. Surrendered. Receptive.

THE
SACRED PATHWAY
TO HEALING CORE
WOUNDS

Your journey is as unique as you are, and there is no time limit set for transformation. And yet, there are certain tangible steps you can choose in order to find acceptance and peace, surrender and empowerment.

Step 1. Understand That None of It Was Your Fault

Practice compassion, loving-kindness, and forgiveness toward yourself.

Step 2. Know Yourself

When you understand your own mystery, purpose, and soul mission, you can step bravely into your empowerment with your story as fuel for wisdom.

Step 3. See Your Mother for Who She Is, Not the Woman You'd Like Her to Be

Mother is a complex archetype and thought-form. Let go of expectations and see your mother as a woman first, systemically programmed within a patriarchal world.

Step 4. Grieve the Absent Mother and the Wounded Child

Allow space for grief and the release of big emotions. Support your Inner Child.

Step 5. Witness and Be Present to Your Wounding, Emotions, and Experiences

Look at what happened honestly and with presence. Witness the pain, and it will witness itself. Fear and anger must have a place to express themselves and dissipate.

Step 6. Find Your Inner Mother and Self-Soothe

Taking responsibility for your own life experience, finding ways to nurture yourself, and shedding the skin of wounding helps you to manifest the life that you want, release your mother from her role as the perpetrator, and cease seeking a "rescuer" relationship, moving from codependence to co-creation.

Step 7.   Build Strong Boundaries

Healthy and strong boundaries with others, and with yourself, protect you from repeating the cycles of abuse, abandonment, and neglect.

Step 8.   Find Support

Seek out supportive relationships with positive people. Find therapy as needed. Avoid drama. Nurture your relationship with the Great Mother.

Step 9.   Know That Healing Is a Spiral

Healing from your mother wound is not a destination; it is a journey of self-discovery and is like any natural cycle that we return to time and again to learn deeper truths, surrender to the process, and grow in wisdom.

At the beginning of your journey to healing, you will awaken to your conditioned self: the one who moves in comfortable and predictable patterns and reactions. You will witness this conditioned self with a desire for change. To meet yourself in this way is challenging. At first, like during stages of grief, you may experience shock and shame.

In the next stage of healing, you become conscious of how you actually co-create your life—that you are not a victim of some mysterious fate, but that you can consciously create your own reality. The conditioned self dissolves some more, taking intentional steps.

Later, you will meet with grief and the Inner Child whose life experiences are those of the individual and the collective.

Throughout the process, we meet surrender—to what was, what is, and what we are creating. As we love ourselves more deeply, with grounded compassion and grace, an acceptance is born.

We live on a deeper level, in a more authentic dimension, where the trauma or wound becomes the gift, serving us and others.

Evidence of Healing

- Feeling at home and safe in your body and in the world.

- Holding memories with courage, love, and compassion instead of fearing them.

- Accepting your mind and thoughts as allies.

- Consistently living in the present moment.

As much as we are individuals,
we are also part of a clan. Like wolves,
women intuitively understand that
connections keep us safe, alive,
and in tune with the greater world.

UNDERSTANDING TRAUMA

Trauma happens when the nervous system is overwhelmed by an experience. It can be brought on by violence, war, attack, accident, verbal or emotional abuse, childhood trauma, the shock of witnessing trauma, and more.

Some of the symptoms of trauma are anger, anxiety, fear, depression, physical manifestations, withdrawal, and thoughts of self-harm.

Trauma is furthered when one's trauma is not acknowledged.

One may get stuck in any of the three stages of trauma: the original shock, the orientation stage (trying to make sense of it), or the initial response to the trauma.

Self-healing or assisted healing consists of several steps:

- **Creating safe space to explore the trauma.**
  This includes gathering resources and tools
  to use along the journey. Resources can be
  somatic practices, relationships, attitudes,
  habits, conditions, and/or qualities.

  *What can help me walk within these shadows
  and stay grounded and stable while I do so?*

- **Exploring the trauma.** The trauma may have
  a size, shape, smell, sound, or color associated
  with it.

  *How does it feel in my body? What do I
  remember, sense, know, or intuit?*

- **Identifying how one could be in positive relationship to the trauma.** Explore the ways in which your trauma might build resilience, safety, and other positive outcomes. Practice loving-kindness toward yourself.

    What can you do now that you could not do before when faced with the memories?

- **Distinguishing between healthy and unhealthy responses.** Pulling in more resources to help yourself understand reactions versus responses.

    Is there something you can research or read about trauma response? Do you need further support from a trauma-informed coach or counselor?

- **Releasing trauma from the body** and recognizing one's resilience and courage is a way to connect the mind, body, and heart.

    How does it feel to know that you have agency over events, memories, and what you keep or let go of?

- **Integrating the experience.** Embodying creative ways to explore and process trauma can result in feelings of self-worth, strength, and peace.

    What has changed in the way you conceptualize trauma and its path in your life?

PART II

First
Steps

"And if we rise up rooted . . . like trees,
well then, women might indeed save not
only themselves but the world."

— SHARON BLACKIE

JOURNAL CREATION

The inner work stemming from these pages may be recorded in a journal of your choosing. A journal is a place where
we meet ourselves having had the courage to put to paper
what matters to our heart.

It is an act of vulnerability and trust, of deep thought
and the desire to preserve your process. By writing, you
pull into the physical world what before was only in the
ether, in the in-between. That's magic!

There is empowerment and healing to be found
through journaling. It is a distinct way of processing whatever your soul and human incarnation are experiencing. It
is as individual as you are.

Journal pages do not judge or expect anything. They
simply exist for the purpose of your expression.

They can be filled with words, art, magazine clippings,
pen, colored pencil or markers, photographs, or colored
yarn. Allow your creativity to play. An online journal is
another alternative, although I encourage you to keep one
in the physical realm so that you can "hold" your journey
in your hands.

You may find, when reading your journal months or
years later, that your wisdom will be so clearly visible, and
you will wonder at the previous you who has now become
your teacher.

Creativity is an inherent part of the Divine Feminine.
This is an excellent way to connect with our own identity
as the Source.

YOUR
GODDESS IMAGE

Flowing further, I invite you to take a photograph of yourself and tuck it into your journal.

What do you feel when you witness the woman looking back at you?

Give yourself permission to play. Adorn yourself in any manner you wish for the photograph, possibly inspired by a goddess of your choosing. Frolic outdoors or inside. This is grounded creative time when you can explore your Self-expression.

Write down the words that flow from Her. Give her voice. As you do, accept that everything she says is simply to be witnessed, not judged. Hold her in your heart space with compassion and love. Your image is the reflection of all women and Goddess herself.

BUILD AN ALTAR

Building an altar grounds your intentions and honors the process you're participating in. Altars connect our collective memory to primal practices, which in ancient times brought us in resonance with the Divine.

Create an area where you can place candles, crystals, a goddess statue to represent Mother, incense, and any other objects special to you and which seem relevant.

You may wish to place a photograph of yourself as a child with or without your mother, a photo of just your mother, or an image of someone who represents your mother on the altar. If you are hearing a resounding *no* to this suggestion, journal it and revisit after the Reconciliation Fire Ritual.

Your altar may change as the months go by. You can add fresh flowers or treasures from the ocean—the womb we all came from—the forest, or the desert. Let this spark your imagination and speak of your story.

Keep this altar alive with light and movement. Take care of it as you would your Inner Child. There is much symbolism and ceremony with altar creation. You are, in fact, creating a new paradigm for your Self.

Notice how the energy of the altar shifts as you do. There will be times of ebb and flow: times when you are inspired by it, and possibly times when you may abandon it. Just observe and journal.

You are energy. Energy must move.

FIND A
MOVEMENT PRACTICE

To help facilitate the movement of your emotions, I suggest that you decide on one physical practice that you will *enjoy*. My favorites are yoga, rebounding, gardening, and nature walks.

What is *your* best, most aligned way of creating movement in your body? Dance, surfing, tennis, bowling, golf, walking your dog, rolling around on the floor . . . there is no wrong way to move.

If you've answered "sex," by the way, then yes! With conscious intention, sex is a sacred medium for soul evolution and a wonderful way to increase endorphins, stop mind-chatter, or move kundalini energy.

SITTING WITH FEAR

by Sarah Norrad

Can we sit with our fear and learn to love it? Can we allow our fear to be a guide to deeper healing?

Because fear is not going anywhere—we can't erase it from our system. Right there in the innate wiring of our nervous system, is programmed our ability to work with fear.

It's a beautiful part of us that we often turn toward in hate; however, fear is a valid piece of our humanness.

The more we fight our fear, the harder it is to process and move forward from. If we don't face our fear, we run from it, or hide it and it becomes our shame.

Can we sit with our fear instead and love it?

Can we use it to remember our wholeness and to remind our Self of our bravery and courage?

Abhaya is a Sanskrit word for fearlessness, which is a goal in both Buddhist and many Hindu paths. It means we do not turn away from things. Instead, we hold a stance of peacefulness and protection toward them.

The problem is not the fear. The problem becomes our avoiding of feelings that we deem as not acceptable. We are always trying to get away from ourselves when something arises that's uncomfortable. What if we loved that piece of discomfort; what if we gave that fear a beautiful embrace of reassurance?

See what happens then?

When we love something, we learn to work with it. Fear does not need to be an obstacle to our sacred healing. Fear can be an anchoring companion to it instead.

Sarah Norrad, certified professional coach

My wings have been there all along, ready to help me take flight from the enveloping shadows. Sometimes the chrysalis, sometimes the butterfly, I am always exactly where I need to be to set my soul free.

PART III

The Alchemy of Words

We are always in transition.
Expecting consistency, predictability,
or a fixed identity produces suffering. Instead,
we can accept the flow of life, letting go of our tight grip
on expectations and releasing the discomfort felt when
we approach inevitable change. Energy cannot bear to be
static. Find beauty in your continually shifting reality.

WRITE YOUR TRANSFORMATION STORY

Spiraling In

You are becoming the alchemist—taking the base metal of wounding and turning it into the gold of self-mastery.

This is sacred work, magical work for mystics and shadow workers—which in fact, we all are, when we open to possibility and spirit.

For some of us, the story is everything. For others, it is a shadow to be forgotten.

You may not entirely remember the story. It may only be surfacing now, or you may have to rely on others to help you put the pieces together. Alternatively, it may be seared with exact precision onto your consciousness. Either way, with the first step taken, you are entering new realms of relating to yourself and the world. There will be defining shifts as the Universe honors your commitment.

Perhaps you recall an incident with your mother that to others may seem insignificant. Or you may be working through the death of your mother at any stage of your life, literal or metaphorical. Wounds cannot be compared, nor can trauma. Each story holds equal value and importance.

You may be surprised at what reveals itself. This course may take you in a direction you could not have expected.

Long-buried codes within our DNA are revealed through conscious introspection.

One thing I do know from doing my own work, is that once you commit to the journey, your cells and psyche will begin their work of releasing. You will begin to dream, lucid dream, and remember in ways you may not expect. People may show up from your past. You may even be visited by the departed, angels, or spirit guides.

All of this is simply an unfolding. It does not even truly matter if you have all the facts straight. We witness ourselves to find compassion for our humanity.

This process is for you. Own it. Watch those wings unfurl!

You must own your story and know that this trauma, this tale, is a portal for finding your purpose, creativity, compassion, and unconditional love.

Wounding exposes your spirit to greater growth. There is always a nugget of purpose embedded in the things we go through. It is for us to uncover and use for the expansion of personal and collective consciousness.

So, while it happened to us, it happened to the whole of Consciousness. We hold the collective wound. When one heals, we all heal. That is a Universal law.

"I'm rewriting my story, and it's beautiful!"

I invite you to surround yourself with anything that brings you joy while you write your story. Find comfortable, inspiring places. Drink your favorite beverage in a special cup. Perhaps take a day to go someplace you consider soulful or healing, such as a garden, or simply spend the day in bed, cradling your Inner Child.

THE ROLE OF THE EGO

You may encounter ego along the road somewhere. Ego may warn you that processing and releasing the story is dangerous. Ego may ask what right you have to go digging through things that obviously will never go away and tell you that you must keep repeating the story, recounting the wounds, or else . . . who would you be without it?

Ego is *not* a self-aware mechanism.

The ego fears death because it cannot imagine life after death—and so it clings. It will try to protect you by convincing you that forgiveness and healing are impossible. You see, to the ego, *transformation means certain death.* Spiritual wisdom acknowledges that life and death are inseparable. If we live, we die; if we die, we live. These cycles are eminent in our lives. We go through many deaths and rebirths during one lifetime. The false safety that the ego provides in this situation is one that keeps us in wound mode if we can't discern the bullshit from the buckwheat.

Ego is an essential part of human life. It keeps us alive in the real world with its freeze, flight, or fight reflex. But when it comes to transformation, it is miserably lost in its own fight for survival.

When the ego and inner critics arrive, treat them with compassion but hold strong boundaries.

After this module, your story may become background information—research material for your soul growth. It will not be something the wound feeds on but learns from. The story is to be honored, valued for its lessons, bathed in light, kept in perspective, and released so the wound can close.

Our wounds are veils or filters through which we
experience our world. They are not who we are.
They are an experience we can move through.

"Who am I without this veil, this story?"

It may come as a surprise that beyond this veil
we are whole. Be curious about yourself, the soul who
is evolving through many lifetimes, many veils.

WRITING PROMPTS

Story I and Story II

Journal your story. You may also paint it, dance it, sing it, play it—or any combination of these modalities.

You may not be able to put it down on paper, yet. Begin where you can.

When you write your story, you are supporting millions of women whose stories have never been heard and who have been silenced forever.

Your Story Is Her Story

What is your mother wound as you conceptualize it in this moment?

Tips for Writing

First person or third person account? You choose. Third person may feel safer at first for some. In a third-person account, you may feel that the distance allows for more perspective, and even more empathy for the situation or persons involved. In first person, you are the narrator, telling the story from your own perspective. In third, your view is not part of the story; you are simply relating events.

The masterpiece is *you*, not the story. Not a writer? No worries. Just write what's in your heart.

Don't agonize over details or flow. Let it come as it wants.

The story may be sparse at first, or full of detail. The goal is to open the container. It is enough.

Story I

To create a consciousness shift around your story—that is, to make a quantum leap from a trauma bond or codependence with trauma, and step out of the triangle of disempowerment between the Perpetrator, the Victim, and the Rescuer—you should write two versions.

Story I is written from the level and archetype of the Serpent. With your belly to the ground, you keep the perspective limited and sensory. This is survival: your freeze, fight, or flight response.

This is the story that the mind and ego are trapped in and which forms emotions to feed the pain.

It looks for a savior or rescuer, which can manifest in the form of a therapist, a lover, or the illusion that one day the perpetrator will be conscious of how they hurt you, apologize, and take responsibility. Or rescue may arrive in the form of an addiction or any number of self-destructive habits, such as believing our own self-deprecating thoughts.

You are in the element of Earth, in the direction of South.

One could begin with:

- *My story is one of narcissistic abuse, abandonment, betrayal, and so on.*

- *The people or person who were part of my present sadness/pain/internalized trauma are . . .*

- *When I was . . . years old, my mother . . .* (Tell the story.)

- *This is not what should have happened. I should have been able to experience . . .* (Insert what you wish life had been like at that time.)

- *I am so angry/sad/hurt/unable to move on.*
  (Name all the ways your human incarnation
  is stuck.)

Or you may imagine another way to begin the story.
Listen to intuition.

You can pinpoint one incident or several that were
key, and which play a major role in your memories, or you
can pick one thing about your mother, father, and grandmother that you find particularly painful or unforgivable,
and which shaped your existence.

You're not trying to figure anything out here or find
resolution. It's simply a story of "this should not have happened"—that is what the mind keeps holding on to. Later
this story will be something that can no longer trigger you
into PTSD states.

Story II

Then we move on to the second story, which has a very
different purpose.

At the end of Story I, ideally, the Serpent sheds her
skin all at once and ceases to identify herself as the victim. She simply leaves the story behind and breaks the
mind's/ego's attachment to it. Then, when sadness arises
over something that happened, you can love that sadness
and have compassion for it instead of joining it on an epic
journey of cellular pain.

Story I is the same story you have lived for many lifetimes, and though you may have learned many lessons
over each lifetime, there is a central theme that is repeated.
This is our three-dimensional (3D) experience.

We can't blame anyone for it. We take responsibility
for our soul's path and the lesson it chose. We also do not

blame ourselves for anything. 3D life is nonsensical to our human perception of logic; but it remains our soul's path to learn through adversity and polarity.

Notice that fairy tales follow this pattern. There is always a poor, helpless person, a "big bad wolf," and a Rescuer. Nothing empowering there.

I personally feel that when we are living our fifth-dimension experience—centered in the heart and intuition—we transcend having to learn from these archetypes through every lifetime.

Story II is the beginning of our 4D/5D experience.

Choose to begin writing Story II now, near the middle, or at the end of this book journey.

In Story II, you are the heroine of your own story. You take responsibility for your own experience. The mind and ego are not fighting with what wasn't fair or who is to blame. One recognizes their story as the absolute perfect occurrence for soul evolution and alchemy.

You are in the element of West. Jaguar. The Luminous Warrior.

You no longer wear your story medicine as armor to protect yourself.

Here are some elements of Story II. You can answer in one sentence or a volume. Speak what needs speaking.

- Where are your ancestors from? Connect with your culture, the wombs you came from, et cetera.

  I was born in . . . , to . . .

- What is your medicine? This could be teaching others through your experience, creativity you have embarked on that facilitates healing for yourself and others—anything you have to offer because of your transformation.

My medicine is . . .

- *But it wasn't always this way . . . . There was a time when . . .*

- In my personal story I wrote, "*I was completely unaware of my place in life. I was an orphan, sexually abused, dissociated . . .*" And on it went. Writing this piece may feel like retreading what happened, but as interesting information: it's the valley you rose from.

- Begin your narrative. The first sentence is often where we get stuck. I suggest a short meditation beforehand to calm the mind and invite inspiration. Relax into the exercise and if nothing is happening, you can return to it when you feel the desire to write.

My story tells . . .

Example: *My story tells the evolution of my soul. It is the path I chose to help me hone the strong medicine I have for the world. I feel so much love and compassion for the courage I have had to live my many lifetimes. Now I know that in order to become the teacher, I have had to be the student and embrace my story as one of the illuminated warriors.*

You can word this in any way you wish or expand on it further.

Example: *I feel called to share my medicine in a humble and powerful way because I understand the pain of many souls and am able to hold them in unconditional love. I am empowered on my chosen path. I understand that my wounding did not happen to me but through me.* (Note that the last sentence shows the transcendence from victim to heroine of your own story.)

Moving Forward: Journal This

- Who will you be without this wound?
- Can you imagine a life where it no longer influences your mood, emotions, physical body, or spiritual awareness? Bring these questions and any insights to your journal.
- Are you thinking of sharing your story?
- If yes, is this the first time you will have shared it?
- With whom will you share it?
- How does it feel to give the story wings?
- Are you sharing it differently than you did or would have before?

Self-Care

- As with any cleansing process, your story may trigger detox symptoms. You are beginning to shed your old skin.
- Drink plenty of water (to help move things through), rest (you may be more tired than usual), allow the tears (honoring emotions), and nourish your body with live, vibrant food.

NINETY-SEVEN

by Tanya Markul

When I realized my pain came from wanting to be liked, I started to love myself.

When I realized my pain came from wanting to be acknowledged, I began to see the woman I really was.

When I realized my pain came from hoping to be special, I set out to explore the depths of my normality.

When I realized my pain came from wanting to be held, I let myself feel the sensations of my body.

When I realized my pain came from craving to belong, I took the first steps to nourish my authentic self.

When I realized my pain originated from the actions of others, I began to accept responsibility for my own story.

When I realized my pain came from chasing those who didn't want me, I set myself free.

Tanya Markul, *The She Book*

The mother wound is the portal for
finding your purpose, creativity, compassion,
and love for others. The story is not the real story.
The real story is your unfolding.

"He who knows others is wise.
He who knows himself is enlightened."

— LAO-TZU

"To know thyself is the beginning of wisdom."

— SOCRATES

PART IV

Know Your Self

I am safe to be in my fullness and take up all the space I need in the world. I am safe to pursue the path I envisioned, desired, and trained for before my incarnation. The whole of the Universe, my guides, and my ancestors support me on my journey.
I embody my purpose.

DISCOVER THE MYSTERY OF YOUR COSMIC SELF

Numerology and *astrology* are powerful tools that can guide you on the journey of self-discovery.

The natural world offers us many signs and systems, which can be viewed as portals to our inner world.

As we are made of the stars, and are ambassadors from other planetary systems to this world, we can take cues from the very mystery of which we are made.

The more we understand the magic of our own incarnation—what planets, moons, and energies work with our personality and soul-designed destiny—the more we can unfold into our sacred journey. Unfolding in this way, we can find the grace, self-forgiveness, and empathy needed to actualize and take full space in our humanity and spirituality.

Further to this, we can understand the Mother archetype and its role in our life. We can answer the unanswerable questions of our past and present. There is a great liberation in understanding Self, a great ownership of our patterns and expectations.

We do not seek to change ourselves, but to befriend and love Self. From this place, we can entertain new visions of growth.

In my *Soul Mission Workbook*, available through my website, monikacarless.com, I outline how to map your soul's desire for this particular incarnation.

If you are working with an astrologer, make sure you find your North Node and South Node, and Moon and Chiron information and placements. These placements most often give insights into core wounds—such as mother wound—their triggers, and can help you understand the path your soul is taking. An excellent North Node book to explore is *Astrology for the Soul* by Jan Spiller.

- **North Node:** The Unknown. Our Soul's Fulfillment, where we lift ourselves to our highest vibration, our Higher Self. It indicates our life purpose in this life. It is where we step into the unknown, being guided by the light of awareness.

- **South Node:** The Known. Issues to complete, closure of old identities. Shows where we may get stuck in old habits that are familiar and comfortable, that were helpful in the past but no longer serve us, baggage from past and present life.

- **Moon:** Mother Aspect. How the moon's placement in our chart influences our emotions and childhood memories. The Mother embodies love, fertility, nourishment, responsibility, patience, power, self-care. She invites you to master giving and receiving love.

- **Chiron:** Placement shows our childhood wounds and the healing that can come of it.

If you are casting your own chart online, use a reliable astrology site. This is a great place to begin until you

find an astrologer whose work and philosophies resonate with you.

- Bring to your journal any newly discovered
  aspects of Self through astrology. Be curious
  about what makes you unique.

- There will never be another human being
  with your unique astrological influences. This
  means that no one else on the planet can
  bring to it what you do. You are mysteriously
  made, and the planets reveal all.

MAJOR LIFE TRANSITS

Another important aspect of knowing ourselves is found through the work of Barbara Hand Clow. She outlines four Major Astrological Life Transits that offer incredible clarity on our evolving consciousness while we are in human form. They are hosted by Saturn, Chiron, and Uranus.

In the past, shamanic societies recognized and celebrated rites of passage within the tribe. We have done away with most rituals initiating us into different stages of life, and have lost the sacredness that comes with recognizing the varied phases a human can pass through.

Concurrently, we have lost touch with, never known, or forgotten the knowledge of key astrological transits through the natal chart, which have a profound effect on our rise in consciousness.

Barbara Hand Clow defines what these transits are, how they affect us, and how we can navigate them for our human and spiritual evolution.

To know which stage one is at or approaching allows for a mindful transit, which can be the difference between life and death, literally or metaphorically. You can discover more in my *Soul Mission Workbook* (monikacarless. com/shop), but here are the main points:

- **Birth to age 30 (First Saturn Return):** This stage includes forming the "I Am" on the physical plane. Saturn asks: *Life or death? What shall we do with our lives? Who shall we mature into?* The Maiden.

- **Age 30 to 42 (Uranus Opposition):** This stage is about perfecting the emotional plane. Some themes are mid-life crisis, kundalini rising, integrating our polar opposite, and stepping into power. The archetype for this transit is the Mother.

- **Age 42 to 50 (Chiron Return):** This stage is about the development of the mind and balance. There is a spiritual awakening at 50, and we become whole. The archetype here is Chiron, the Wounded Healer.

- **Age 58 to 60 (Second Saturn Return):** This stage is about stepping into wisdom. Another chance to unfold into purpose, with the Eros/ Death theme revisited. The archetype for this transit is the Crone.

For other important transits, and more detail on each life period, I recommend *Astrology and the Rising of Kundalini* by Barbara Hand Clow.

CHARTING YOUR COURSE

*"We meet ourselves time and time again in
a thousand guises on the paths of life."*

— CARL JUNG

There are many roads that one can take, many ways to find creative expression of Self, and none of those roads are wrong. All roads taken are some forms of self-discovery.

According to numerology, Pythagorean mysticism/ philosophy, and sacred geometry, we are inherently designed to embody certain desires, traits, and journeys.

In this way, the Universe discovers itself and creates through our experiences. And in this way, *we* discover the Universe within Self.

Knowing our life path, soul urge, and destiny numbers and their meanings can help illuminate the dark corners of why we're here. You can find online calculators for these, or decipher them on your own, then look up the meanings.

I recommend *The Life You Were Born to Live* by Dan Millman for a more in-depth study of your life path number as well as the numerology for your family and friends. Otherwise, work with a numerologist or consult with online interpretations and numerology books.

*"What lies before us and what lies behind us are
small matters compared to what lies within us.
And when we bring what lies within out into
the world, miracles happen."*

— HENRY DAVID THOREAU

Find Your Birth Number by Your Own Calculation

First, start with your birthdate: Month/Day/Year.

Example: 11/04/1972

Then, reduce the month, day, and year down to a single digit by adding them.

Example: 1+1+4+1+9+7+2 = 25 = 2+5 = 7

Life path #7

By this calculation, your Life Path Map to explore in Dan Millman's book would be 25/7. Any numerology app can help guide your way too.

GETTING TO KNOW YOUR MOTHER

Exploring your mother's birth date, tarot influence, sun sign, and life path number is an approach you may already have or could find helpful.

Just as knowing ourselves leads to true embodiment, knowing the woman whose womb birthed us can lead to greater self-understanding (where you came from), self-love (what happened has many roots), and a dissolution of anger, grudges, and blame.

It can lead to compassionate dialogue, even forgiveness.

At the least, it will shed light onto the path before you. At most, it will free you.

Witness your mother's journey.

Enter into this gently. Our mind wants to cling to the pain, because, as we discussed before, the ego resists transformation. But with an intentional and compassionate exploration, you can see your mother with more clarity.

CHARTING A NEW COURSE

In charting a new course, you are pulling together all the information you have gathered about yourself. From this perspective, you witness a new understanding of yourself in relation to how you now understand your mother. You're standing in your authentic journey and giving Mother space for hers. You can identify which astrological transit you are living through now. You can perhaps recall major events that happened at different stages of your life in relation to those transits, and which numbers influence your current incarnation.

- What have you discovered about yourself through your birth chart that helps you understand your choices, thoughts, and inclinations? Perhaps you have had a birth chart reading previously. Do you have new insights through another look?

- Does this inspire you to have more compassion for yourself and to see your journey with more introspection? How?

- How does knowing your mother's life path number allow for better understanding of her as a woman on her own journey, and how does it compare to yours? Do her choices make more sense now?

- Intuit into your body and recognize how it felt to read about her life path number influences. What came up? Understanding or judgment? (Do not judge the reaction, simply observe.)

- Delve deeper into the numbers and astrology. Perhaps create a colorful art board depicting yourself as your sun sign and planet placements. You can also depict your personal numerology with symbolism, such as tarot card or runes that correspond to your life path number, or even just the number itself, which will carry its resonance to the art board. Include a poem or thought you have written to yourself.

- Do you wish to include your mother and her influences in this art project, or do you wish to journey alone? Can you sense where you are headed? Let your intuition guide who this space is for.

PART V

The Mother Archetype

Empowered.
I am not a victim of circumstance.
I claim my sovereignty and agency.
I claim choice and my voice.
I take personal responsibility for
the choices I make.

"The birth mother is always the death mother and vice-versa.

— CLARISSA PINKOLA ESTÉS

THE GREAT MOTHER

*"'Mother' is a complex and deeply
mystical thought-form."*

— CARL JUNG

Carl Jung considered the Mother archetype most important
of all because it seemed to encompass all other archetypes.

Archetypes are defined as universal thought-forms
or mental images that influence an individual's feelings
and actions.

We become familiar with archetypes very early on,
through fairy tales, myths, or religions, and through
dreams and cultural stories. Contained within the collective unconscious, archetypes help us make sense of our
outer world and the mysteries of the cosmos and nature—
which, paradoxically, helps us to make sense of our inner
world. To actualize Self and our personal purpose on
earth, we must ironically venture beyond Self and delve
into Collective Wisdom. Archetypes help us to understand
the human consciousness and psyche.

We are born of the womb, a dark, primordial space
within which all of creation manifests. It is literal and
metaphorical. It is the ocean, from where all life evolved.
It is the Void, from which the Universe unfolded. It is comforting, warm, nourishing, safe, and dark.

It is in darkness that we are formed and through darkness that we *transform*. It is our mother's womb. We are, as
a species, hardwired for Mother.

Through religion, we learn of the saintly mother. The good mother. The impossibly perfect mother. Through fairy tales, we meet the dark mother, the stepmother, the incapable mother—and sometimes the good mother, but she always seems to die early on leaving us to learn the harsh realities of life. (Sometimes the fairy godmother steps into her role. Other times, we are rescued from the bad mother by a masculine figure.)

As a collective consciousness, we have great expectations of Mother as well as the Divine Masculine, which forms a basis of codependence.

The truth is, our mother often does not live up to our expectations. We may mistake our mother for the archetypal ideal. She is a reflection of the Great Mother, and to understand her we need to understand the Great Mother and *her* wound.

MOTHER AS MYSTERY

Goddess takes many forms.

She is manifested in the Great Mother (Creatress), in Gaia (Mother Nature), and in Divine Feminine energy and expression (present in all genders). She is birthed from the Spirit realm to the physical world via woman (who becomes Mother and is likewise, daughter).

The mystery of the Triple Goddess—Maiden, Mother, Crone—is reflected in the phases of the moon and the cycles of birth, life, death, and rebirth.

Woman is the mystery physically representing the Great Mother, the Divine Feminine, and the Triple Goddess.

She, like nature, can create, sustain, *and* destroy. Sometimes she is the gentle rain, sometimes the monsoon. Sometimes the quiet river, sometimes the tsunami. Sometimes sunshine, sometimes thunder. She is ever evolving, and is sometimes the earthquake.

She gives us our footing and then requires us to find our own. When we see Mother as a mirror for nature, and nature as a mirror for Mother, we understand that Mother is not always *safe mother*.

Safe mother would do it all for us, and therefore, keep us from spreading our wings. Life would be very one-dimensional, and we would never understand how to interpret danger if living with a *too-safe* mother. We would trust every stranger that came along, because safe mother does not teach us to trust our intuition.

Many daughters have said that they felt their whole life was about *surviving* their mother.

And should we dig deeper still, the root of the struggle is with the Great Mother, Goddess, Nature herself, because within our centuries' old survival instinct, we have felt abandoned by Goddess and by our mother planet through many natural disasters, famines, and shifts in Her body.

Sadly, the Great Mother also carries the collective wound of human impact upon her soil and oceans. Every act of ecocide carried out against the Great Mother is embodied by Woman. Every act of violence against women since the beginning of time is carried within the cell memory and DNA of Woman. Our suffering and healing are intertwined.

Healing the mother wound is deeply personal yet gives rise to a stronger community worldwide.

The Great Mother, the Divine Feminine, and Woman, long in conflict with the shadow side of the Divine Masculine (the patriarchy), has had to withdraw from her inherent nature to survive.

She . . .

- has rejected her instincts and intuition

- has hidden and denied her wisdom

- has abandoned herself and her dreams

- may not fit the role of Mother and Divine Feminine as outlined by society

- has not held her Self or been able to nurture her vulnerable Inner Child

- has given in to her own rage at her inability to rise sovereign

- has been deemed hysterical, unstable, untrustworthy, crazy, too emotional, too much, too little

- has endured medical interference with her cycles and birthing process, and has been given unnecessary surgeries and hormonal disruptors aimed at keeping her wild nature at bay

- has been told to mind her mouth

- has been raped, burned, and drowned. Her lakes, rivers, oceans, forests, and farmlands have been systematically destroyed.

- has directed her unhappiness and lack of purpose at her mirror image, her daughter. Nature, the Divine Feminine, and Woman have become "resources" to be exploited.

Such denial of Self builds grief and rage. Rage creates wildfires and tsunamis. Rage creates mothers who cannot support the life they gave birth to. Grief consumes everything in its path.

At some point along the way, often at too young an age, we begin to absorb our mother's pain. We take it on as our own. We don't trust our intuition. We doubt our wisdom. We attract partners who mirror our lack of self-love. We don't trust our emotions. The cycle continues.

Empowerment lies in the awareness that our
unhappiness is not the responsibility of our mother.
Unhappiness may stem from our relationship with
mother, but it is our own responsibility.
Reframed, we can own our rising, free from the
tether to which we had enslaved ourselves.

WHAT IS MOTHER?

The Road to Restoration

Mother is all things, just as the Great Mother is all things.

She is the kind, nurturing woman, the white witch, the kind, wise queen, and the innocent princess. She is Luna, lighting our path.

She is the hag, the dark witch, the angry, jealous queen, and the destructive force of nature. She is Kali, breathing fire.

As soon as we see Mother in all her versions, we can find compassion for the woman who, through her incarnation as the Divine Feminine, mirrors the complexity of the Goddess.

As soon as we give up the fantasy of the "good mother," we can embrace the light and shadow within *ourselves* and further, within our own mother.

The destruction of Woman as healer, creatress, sorceress, wise woman, alchemist, and birther of consciousness has led to detachment from Self and purpose.

This is ours to rebirth and resurrect within us through healing our mother wound.

THE INVITATION

The invitation is to witness your mother as these archetypes:

- Goddess
- Wise Woman
- Healer
- Creatress

When you witness someone, you are giving space for their joy, their pain, their successes, their failures, their light, and their dark. You are honoring their beingness in the same way you wish to be honored.

- In meditation or reflection, allow an image of the archetypal Woman to come to mind. See her in the way she has been unseen and unheard through millennia. There is a natural compassion for Woman because she is you and you are her. To support her is to support yourself. The time is now, on the planet, for women to stand together and reclaim their magic.

- Imagine now your mother merging with Woman: her face is the face of all women. She is the embodiment of all the healing that must occur within the Mother archetype. Witness your mother.

If you can envision it, look into her eyes. See the woman, the Divine Feminine, the Great Mother, and Goddess.

- As you do this, you are also peering into your own consciousness and humanity. See yourself as the Divine Feminine, the Great Mother, and Goddess.

A SHAMANIC RITUAL

Mother as Avatar for Woman

In the spirit of sisterhood, within the meditation realm, invite the archetypal Woman as your mother to a virtual healing circle.

This embodiment exercise is meant to take place within the spirit realm, but if your heart is calling for a physical healing circle, then by all means, invite your mother to join you.

Gather some or all of the following items: meditation/circle dance music; a drum, tambourine, rattle, or any instrument of your choice; and your journal. Take a seat near your altar.

- Light the candles on your altar, get comfortable, and let yourself fall into the music you have chosen.

- Close your eyes and silently imagine witnessing each other through your Third Eye. Imagine the journey of Woman through time, all she has endured and survived. Extend blessings to her, thanking her for her strength and fortitude, for her tears and her wisdom.

- Imagine that you are making an offering to Woman. A gift of a shell or a raven feather—anything that comes to mind.

Or you can place something on your altar as an actual gift.

- Accept any gift she may have for you. Acknowledge that she is another you and you are another her.

- Now, as the two of you join for a sacred circle dance, other women begin to appear, women from many lifetimes, your ancestry, and all tribes. You begin to dance together and play your instruments. You offer laughter and support. You visualize your mother melting into the many women around the circle. She, and you, are the women who are beginning to remember.

- Recite these words:

    "Wise One, Healer, Lover, Mother, Sister, Daughter, Creatress, Aunt, Inner Child, Witch, Luna, Kali, Divine Feminine, Goddess.
    "This is the awakening."

- Dance for as long as you wish, connecting through your imagination to all the women you have invited to your circle. Make note of and journal the following in your own time:

    Who comes?
    Who sits on the side, afraid to participate?
    Who succumbs to tears?
    Who softens?
    What gifts are shared?
    Who hardens?
    Who leaves?

- End your dance by passing an imaginary
  or real squeeze of the hand beginning with
  you and ending with you. Each squeeze is
  accompanied by the mantra:

  *"I witness you as you are. I love you as
  you are."*

  Know that as you say these words you are
  also saying them to yourself.
- Release Woman/your mother and all the
  women in the circle into the spirit realm.

- Finish the meditation in Child's Pose if able.
  This is a perfect pose for surrendering to
  the journey you are on. It is a place of no-
  thought. It elongates the spine, moving spinal
  fluid or kundalini energy from the base to
  your brain; it also stretches the hips, where
  we hold emotions and trauma. Child's Pose
  symbolizes resting in what is.

WITNESSING MOTHER IN HER MANY FORMS

The following is an excerpt from my Wise Woman Mystery School.

Mother Is Home

To tap into the Mother archetype is to find our way back home, to before our incarnation, to the place where our soul came from (our spiritual Self), and it is also honoring our human self.

There are times when we feel lost, ungrounded, and yearning for something undefined. What we search for is wholeness.

Through daily life, we scatter bits of ourselves in many different directions. Mother archetype can help us bring those pieces back together.

- Choose a sunny day and find a spot in nature that feels supportive and safe.

- Bring a blanket, some of your favorite comfort food, a flask of tea or coffee, your journal, and some magical items from your altar, plus a gift for Mother Earth.

- Take a few moments to settle, notice the beauty around you, and sit in gratitude for your surroundings and being able to take this time to yourself.

- Lie down on the earth. Feel her beneath you, supporting and loving you. Sink your bones deeply; imagine growing roots.

- Now visualize the pieces you have lost to worry, anger, fear, and circumstance.

- Imagine a compassionate, loving, mother figure helping you gather these pieces and handing them to you. Imagine her placing her hands over your heart as you breathe yourself back together. Take your time in this magical place.

- Feel the generosity and wholeness she provides. Allow yourself to receive and integrate. Stay here for a while.

- Open your eyes when you feel complete.

- Look around you. Does the world look different? How do you feel? Indulge in your picnic. When leaving, place your gift somewhere inconspicuous for Mother Earth.

An Abundance/Reciprocity Meditation

- Open your arms wide, pull your spine up straight, and breathe in deeply.

- Take a moment to *feel* your hands—become aware of them as part of you.

- Visualize your heart opening wide. Take a moment. Feel it.

- Receive the energy of abundance through your left palm. Allow it to travel up your arm to your heart.

- Take a moment for your heart to fill with gratitude. Feel the abundance.

- Continue the flow down your right arm, to your right palm.

- Bring your hands together at your heart center, transferring the energy back to your left palm.

- Repeat as many times as you wish.

Finding a Gift for Mother

Which Mother would you like to share a gift with? Choose between Mother Nature, your mother, or a mother figure. A gift for yourself closes the circle as you validate your role in representing the Great Mother.

Have fun with the gift. It could be something small, like a crystal, pebble, or feather; or it could be something more expansive, like planting a tree, creating a craft from natural elements, or writing a song.

Continue with your movement practice. Are you seeing a flow of energy that wasn't there before as a result of your practice?

Self-embodiment is a woman's pilgrimage home.

MOTHER ARCHETYPE
AND PATRIARCHY

*"Civilized Man says: I am Self, I am Master,
all the rest is other—outside, below, underneath,
subservient. I own, I use, I explore, I exploit, I control.
What I do is what matters. What I want is what matter
is for. I am that I am, and the rest is women and
wilderness, to be used as I see fit."*

— URSULA K. LE GUIN

*"No male successfully measures up to
patriarchal standards without engaging in an
ongoing practice of self-betrayal."*

— BELL HOOKS

In sharing these two quotes, I suggest that it is the shadow side of the Divine Masculine that has long participated in destroying the sovereignty and well-being of Woman, Gaia, and reverence for the Great Mother, as embodied by the Mother archetype.

In order for a person identifying as male (or equally, a person identifying as female) to engage with patriarchal energy, they must first betray their beginnings as an incarnated impulse of love.

Since the beginning of time, Woman has created magic and healing, and held space and honed her intuition, by using what the Great Mother offered naturally: sticks, stones, and the alchemy of her love.

Her wisdom has been driven underground through the distortion and dissonance of patriarchy. She now seeks new ground, rising, rebirthing, and awakening.

Healing the mother wound births new paradigms and restructures our DNA and the DNA of consciousness.

It challenges patriarchy at its core. Yes, we, as individuals can create massive shifts in the fabric of societal evolution by addressing how patriarchy has affected our mother-lines.

The Role of Patriarchy within the Mother Archetype

Sociologist Sylvia Walby describes *patriarchy* as "a system of social structures and practices in which men dominate, oppress, and exploit women."

Through many social systems and institutions developed over time—religious, educational, etc.—both men and women have embodied patriarchy.

The Mother archetype, which shape-shifts according to the energy of the age we are in (currently shifting from Piscean to Age of Aquarius), realizes that the domination of women and the planet is a system that can be re-created into a healthy one.

The Piscean Age, from A.D. 1 to A.D. 2000, is represented by the solar plexus chakra—power, ego, control, and hierarchy.

The Age of Aquarius, from A.D. 2000 to A.D. 4000, is represented by the heart chakra—love, service, harmony, freedom, and equality.

There have been many positive aspects of the Piscean Age, such as developments in artistry and spirituality (this is the Age of Jesus—so much to do with the element of water), as well as advancements in technology; but most of it was led and recorded through *his-story*.

As the Age of Aquarius began its initial influence a few centuries ago, it sought a balancing of the predominantly masculine energy on the planet, and we began to see the rise of gentler, more inclusive movements.

- *Aspects of the Masculine*: expressive, decisive, concrete, assertive

- *Aspects of the Feminine*: intuitive, abstract, tranquil, receptive

In balance, they push a society to evolve toward heart-based philosophies.

The Divine Feminine, the Great Mother, Gaia, and Woman, rises as she is called to the service of humanity.

The work of healing the mother wound is the work of many hearts joined in ushering in the Age of Aquarius.

We heal to live through the heart,
so the whole of society can live through the heart.

Note: Patriarchy can be embodied by a person of any gender. It does not only evolve through the visually masculine, because the Masculine, just as the Feminine, is an integral part of all beings. To dismantle patriarchy, we must be willing to look at where it lives within ourselves and be willing to dismantle the shadows of dominance and subjugation.

Dreaming a New Age: Exploring How Patriarchy Influenced Your Story

The Immature Masculine, disconnected from his vulnerability and ability to express his emotions, unsupported in his emotional development by Mother, and trained into manhood by a misogynistic society and Father, lashes out at all that represents the Feminine: intuition, and what he deems as the chaos of female emotions.

Awed by the Feminine's ability to birth all of humanity and bring Spirit into human form by the magic of her blood and womb, Father seeks to engage with blood alchemy, but he can only do so through shedding it in war and aggression. He draws his false power through violence, oppression, and domination. Disconnected from the responsibility of his actions, he is unrepentant and unaware of his privilege.

In his primary relationship with Mother, he remains an infant who at once seeks the comfort of what she represents (this includes all of nature, the planet, and its resources) and at the same time holds great disrespect for her gifts, expressing his disrespect through his relationships with partners, children, and his environment.

Men who live through the heart create the template for men who through their conditioning, cannot access their vulnerability and compassion.

Women who have the support of their partners to raise vulnerable, compassionate sons create a new heart template for the Aquarian Man.

The Aquarian Man can participate in supporting the Divine Feminine in her role as Mother/Daughter. The Mother archetype evolves toward 5D Consciousness.

Your mother-line, steeped for centuries in the pre-dominant philosophy of the Piscean Age, has sometimes willingly or unwillingly participated in misogyny and patriarchy and the fallout of that on your own story. As Lucy H. Pearce wrote in *Burning Woman*:

> As Burning Women, our maternal lines prob-ably go back through many, many women who shut down to their fire, were burned by others, and whose fires burned them, their families, and their marriages alive. We are the descendants of grand-mothers and mothers who each handled the fire in their own way, trying to survive.

Exploring Patriarchy within Your Mother-Line

- Where in your story do you see influences of patriarchy and misogyny, and did it create a disconnect within the mother/daughter relationship directly or indirectly?

- Can you see how your mother and/or grandmother took on the philosophy and actions of the patriarchy within your family, perhaps not embodying the Feminine but subjugating to the will of the Immature Masculine in their actions and thought patterns? How did this affect how they mothered you?

- Do you think they were aware of this influence on their life or even had the clarity to think this through, or were they acting in survival mode as women within a patriarchal society?

- As women who were most likely not seen or heard, did they pass on their frustration and anger to the next generation? How so within your own story?

- Can you give an example(s) how you may have continued this cycle or ways you did not?

- What new processes can you implement within your own life and that of your family that support the Divine Feminine and the Mother archetype in healing the collective mother wound?

- What wisdom can you pass on to your children or your younger, present, or future Self that will guide your healing and actions?

- How has your mother's fire been doused by patriarchy? Give any examples you can think of. Can you stand in compassion for this woman stripped of her power and her fire?

- What can you offer her in words to show her that you witness her inability to rise above those circumstances and the choices she made within those circumstances?

- Write a message or letter to express your emotions about this—where the pain lies.

- What are some ways you can claim back your own power, which may have been taken away through patriarchy?

When we show understanding and compassion
for the women before us who embodied patriarchy and
misogyny, we are not condoning their choices or actions,
but are standing with all women who lived with their
power unexpressed in positive ways.
We own our pain and our disappointment,
while simultaneously giving voice to it as we write,
speak, paint, or dance it. When we claim our
freedom from patriarchal thought or action,
we claim it for all women.

*"We can use our difficulties and
problems to awaken our hearts."*

— PEMA CHÖDRÖN

PART VI

Chakra Alignment

*The first goddess whose magic and influence
we become intimate with is the woman
whose womb we chose.*

*Mother becomes the source, physically, emotionally,
and spiritually. Our relationship with the Goddess
is woven alongside our relationship with Mother.*

BASE AND 10TH CHAKRAS

While in utero, we absorb our mother's emotions and her addictions (physical and emotional). We are already borrowing from our mother's experience and adopting it into our own psychology. We learn by example and mirror the one whose heartbeat has been our sole companion for the first nine months of life.

Once out into the physical world, as the ego begins the work of evolving the personality, we encounter our mother's sense of worthiness (or lack thereof) as well as her ego. The infant does not recognize that they are separate from mother. We begin the dance of pleasing her while continuing to find our own ground. Childhood never seems to end when in relationship with our mother. Do you notice that her presence, her memory, or her words can quickly rip away a carefully built footing? This is where the work lies—stone by stone, taking down the walls of codependence.

Base chakra strength is the foundation upon which we build our whole physical existence. It rebuilds our foundation with tools that remind us of our sovereignty and reason for being.

Common Symptoms of Base Chakra Misalignment

Symptoms may ebb and flow throughout your life, decreasing or increasing with circumstances or the ability to work on these shadows, or there may be one predominant symptom. You may recognize some that have been resolved and others that show up with consistency.

Awareness is key as some symptoms shape-shift into illness, or we keep running into others who mirror the symptoms to us when we can't see them within ourselves.

- Lack of self-trust, trusting others, trusting life itself
- Inability to build and maintain healthy boundaries
- Choosing unsupportive relationships or situations
- Lack of self-love and self-appreciation
- Difficulty aligning heart and throat chakras
- Resistance to forgiveness and letting go of resentments
- Feeling unsupported by the Universe
- Fear is a common motivating factor as opposed to faith
- Lack of self-confidence
- Perpetuating the cycle we learned during childhood

When a child finds home, safety, and love in relationship with a mother who is confident in her role as nurturer for the life she has birthed, the child can build her own sense of self and confidence upon this foundation. A child who cannot find that healthy attachment develops unhealthy attachments wherever she may find them. The wounded mother may even desire or try her best to provide healthy attachment but may not have the emotional tools or be grounded enough herself to be that positive influence.

Base Chakra Correspondences

Sanskrit name: Muladhara, or *root support*

Element: Earth

Location: Base of spine, tailbone, between the anus and genitals

Color: Red

Deals with: Security, survival instinct, fear and abundance, tribe, embodiment

Purpose: A link for the Spiritual Being to the material/physical world. Serves as the basis for the evolution of the personality and self-expression.

Symbol: Four-petaled lotus

Essential Oils: Cedar, myrrh, clove, marjoram

Gemstones: Garnet, ruby, bloodstone, smoky quartz, black tourmaline, black onyx plus other black, dark, or reddish stones

Planets and Zodiac: Mars, Scorpio, Capricorn, Saturn, Aries, Taurus

Glands: Adrenals

Body Parts: Bones, teeth, prostate, limbs, nails, intestines

In alignment, Self can focus on expansion, embodiment, manifesting a desired earth experience, and a connection with the Great Mother—with nature and her cycles.

Out of alignment, life is viewed through a lens of fear and insecurity and becomes a basic fight for survival. Stress becomes a common cause of illness. One may not trust society or authority in general, and most poignantly, not trust Self. There may also be an inability to trust nature and a focus on material possessions.

Strategies for Grounding

- Eat grounding foods: root vegetables, meat, beans, grains.

- Walk barefoot.

- Use the color red in clothing and home surroundings.

- Use crystals and essential oils on the body, in meditation or healing rituals.

- Practice rituals that have meaning to you. One suggestion is a tea ritual with mindful attention to details such as the cups used, the time taken to brew the tea, the aroma of the tea, and reverent action of pouring the tea. Ritual-making is a calming, centering activity practiced within many cultures and religions because of its ability to align the base chakra with the intention of the activity.

- Connect with nature, the Great Mother, regularly.

- Drink plenty of good water.

- Swim or lie in moving bodies of water, or alternatively, soak in the water of a bath or shower. Walk in the rain. The negative ions emitted during a rainstorm clear negativity.

- Meditate. Allow for stillness and silence.

- Follow the cycles of the moon, planets, and seasons.

- Journal. The practice of writing or recording events, thoughts, and emotions connects your spirit with the physical realm.

- Lie naked on the earth.

- Choose "I am" statements as daily affirmations for full embodiment. The base chakra resonates deeply with the mantra *I Am*. It is an energetic place of calm and grounding.

Where Is the 10th Chakra?

Chakras 1 through 7 reside within the body. Outside the body and directly above the crown chakra are:

Number 8 – Connection to the Divine

Number 9 – The Seat of the Soul

Number 11 – Mind over Matter

Number 12 – Universal Unity

There are three schools of thought as to where the 10th chakra is. One is 1.5 feet below your feet/the earth, another locates it at 3 feet below, and yet another has it above the crown between the 9th and 11th chakras.

My pagan tradition recognizes it as anywhere between 1.5 and 3 feet below the earth. We'll be working with that premise and intention here.

Our chakras connect us with the Seat of Creation. Imagine an energetic cord grounding us to Mother Earth all the way through our lower body and up through the crown, to the ether, the stars, and outer space. Our One-ness is manifested through this system, and it's how we're all energetically woven into the same tapestry of life.

Why is it important for everyone, and especially empaths and Highly Sensitive People, to ground them-selves through the 10th chakra?

Empaths and HSPs need regular grounding and solid-ifying into their physical bodies. Because we work daily with unseen energies and tend to absorb them (even with rock-solid boundaries), it is necessary to continually rein-force our human, physical aspect.

Many Empaths, Light-workers, and spiritually inclined people wish to escape their human container and "reality" in the belief that the body is an encumbrance to their spir-itual ascension.

But this creates a lot of problems and blockages in the other chakras because we incarnated with the specific intent to be human; therefore, being chronically ungrounded, (floating in the ether) is a pathway to depression, dissolu-tion about one's purpose, chronic pain, and illness.

Connecting to the 10th chakra with the intent of empowering one's physical incarnation leads to harmony and vibrancy on all other chakra levels.

The 10th chakra embodies:

- The energy of the earth
- The balancing of the Divine Feminine and Divine Masculine aspects
- Connection to the Elemental Kingdom (fey, crystals)

- Remembering talents, gifts, and wisdom from previous lives
- Connection to ancestors
- Synchronicity and creativity
- 12-strand DNA activation
- The symbiotic relationship between Light and Dark, as the 10th and 12th chakras are directly linked. They mirror each other in a similar way that Twin Flames do on their soul journey.

As much as this chakra is earthy and dark, it actually amplifies light.

Earth elements that may be used to support the 10th chakra are any black stones such as hematite, black onyx, black tourmaline, lava rock, schungite, as well as amber (fossil), jasper, and clear quartz to amplify those stones.

I also like to use essential oils during meditation or in my everyday with the 10th chakra, such as cedarwood, frankincense, sandalwood, patchouli, vanilla and balsam.

The Meditation

A common way of grounding is to pull energy down from crown chakra to the root and then leave it at that. It is necessary, however, to afterward bring that grounding back up through the body to fortify all the chakras with earth energy. The stillness and rootedness are then in harmony with Spirit and can be offered back to the Universe. As above, so below. Alchemy of the soul. You can record this meditation first and play it back as needed.

- Sit in a chair or on a meditation cushion with your feet planted firmly on the ground.

- Spend a few moments in gratitude for the earth, which supports you and the life you came to live.

- Think of a place on Earth that is special to you. This may be a place you have visited in this or another lifetime or wish to go to in the future. It may be your garden space, the local park, or any patch of earth that brings you joy.

- Take three deep breaths in and out, releasing tension and breathing in peaceful harmony, allowing your thoughts to settle, and observing quietly how they dissipate. Don't judge any of those thoughts, just observe and allow them to pass through.

- Imagine reaching your energy high above you into the cosmos and bringing that star energy down. Allow it to fill the 12th chakra very slowly. When you are ready, let it filter down through the 11th, the 9th, then the 8th. This light resonates with the fullness of your Inner Being.

- Open your crown chakra like a lotus flower in bloom, and allow that spirit-infused light to fill every nook and cranny of your brain. Let it nourish your Third Eye, awakening your intuition, your throat, and your Truth. Let it illuminate your neck and shoulders, and then embrace your heart chakra, your whole chest, and your arms down to your fingertips.

- Slowly, slowly, slower yet, let this light
  fill your solar plexus, awakening personal
  power, your lower abdomen, your legs, and
  your root chakra in waves of radiating,
  empowering light. Let this light power your
  soul and creativity.

- Allow yourself time to truly relax and enjoy
  this process—to fill up and fuel up. Take as
  long as you wish; there is no time limit on
  this meditation. Let this be a retreat into
  your stillness. Remember your desire to visit
  the earth in a human body and embrace the
  journey you are on. You are a magical being
  on a purpose-filled mission.

- From the bottom of your feet, imagine the
  ground opening beneath you, allowing you
  to find the earth's comforting, unconditional
  embrace. Surrender to the love of the Great
  Mother. Feel her compassion. Feel her wisdom.
  Find a path among the roots of the Tree of Life.
  In the Underworld, there is full acceptance of
  your unique journey on the earth.

- Deeper, deeper, deeper yet. Make yourself a
  nest among the roots, line it with soft moss,
  and feel the warmth of your safe place.
  Breathe slowly. Notice the scent of forest,
  leaves, and soil. Notice now that you are
  growing roots as well. These roots spread wide
  and deep into the earth beneath you. You are
  grounded in the womb of the Goddess.

- You feel supported and seen. You can now bring this feeling of rootedness and grounding up through your feet to center your base chakra. As you bring this peaceful, rooted energy up through your 7 chakras, they begin to spin clockwise in perfect harmony with each other and your purpose on earth.

- You feel incredibly strong of heart. You feel loved and accepted and in turn love and accept others.

- Offer this rootedness to flow upward into the cosmos as an offering. Place your hands on the ground and feel the "earth" beneath you. Share words of gratitude for the Great Mother. Rub your hands briskly together in front of your heart center. Feel the warmth. Keeping your hands in prayer mudra, raise them to your Third Eye.

YOUR PERSONAL ARCHETYPES

Everyone has personal archetypes that reveal their purpose and are the seeds from which they can expand into full embodiment during each incarnation.

We experience our incarnations simultaneously, although we are taught that they progress linearly. We draw from all our incarnations to bring our specific gifts to the world.

In this exercise, you will engage intuition to discover and remember your personal archetypes.

In your meditation space, however you wish to create that—maybe in the traditional way, or sitting with your back against your favorite tree, or in a cafe with a delicious coffee and pastry—journal all the archetypes that you feel you are embodying during this lifetime. You will notice that some are in seed form, some are emerging, and some have fully awoken.

Example: Some of my archetypes are Creative, Earth Keeper, Priestess, Rebel, Revolutionary, Bridge Between Worlds, Explorer, Witch, Old Soul, Community Builder, and EcoActivist.

Write all that comes to heart for you. Be bold! Don't edit. Let it free flow. There may be 5 or 40.

Some will feel comfortable, some may be joyful, some may be fearful, and some will make you laugh out loud. Performer made me laugh, for instance. Not comfortable at all, and yet . . .

In the months to come, you can return to this exercise and see in which ways you have grown, embodied, expanded, run away, et cetera. The archetypes that induce fear are the ones that will help you step into full embodiment as you face that shadow.

Where do you feel joy as you explore your archetypes? These are the juicy places of your being that are alive within you now and you are ready to dive into deeply.

We can heal our wounds by listening to each other's stories.

PART VII

Meeting Your Mother-Line

The mother wound is infused with fear
of our own power, with our mother's
fear of her power, and her mother's fear.
When we rise from the waters of our own fears,
we slay the dragons of our mother-lines.
We heal many generations to come.

Relate to your mother,
not as your Inner Child,
but as an adult.

Watch the dynamic between you
shift dramatically and the doors
to healing open.

ANCESTRAL HEALING AND RECONCILIATION

Who is she? Who am I? Who were they? Who are we?

These four questions form the basis of the exploration into your mother-line. We are connected womb-to-womb, dream-to-dream, hope-to-hope, life-to-life, and often, wound-to-wound.

Why should we dig beyond ourselves to heal the mother wound?

Every woman—every grandmother, mother, and daughter—craves to be seen. Exploring our mother-line is much like travel to another culture. It opens our eyes to experiences beyond our own. It also allows previous generations and the women who came before us to be witnessed while observing ourselves within that ancestral tapestry.

We are all connected through the alchemy of DNA, blood, and embryonic fluid in which we floated and steeped. Many wombs have supported us through centuries of births and rebirths.

We live our entire lives—past, present, and future—at once, and while it's difficult to understand that concept of overlapping time, it allows us an idea of just how important our shadow work is: We heal all layers, including those of our ancestors and our children, when we walk through the fires of personal transformation.

Gathering Stories

Our stories and the stories of women across the ages can empower a shift in human consciousness. These stories have been stored in our collective memory, so often snuffed out as women's voices have been silenced.

What is so important is that we give voice to ourselves and to the women before us.

Before we can do that, we must know who those women were, and how we came to grow from their experience and their ancestral wombs.

As much as we are individuals, we are also part of the clan. Like wolves, women intuitively understand that connections keep us safe, alive, and in tune with the greater world in which we live. To know our mother-line is to tap into a deeper knowing of ourselves and the Great Mother. She lives and breathes through us all.

Embark on a Small or Big Project Tracing Your Mother-line

When we see ourselves through the lens of the women who came before us, we can begin to heal what flows through us consciously.

The following are four practices to connect you with your near or far, alive or transitioned ancestors, and center you in the practical work of healing and reconciliation.

- What is your personal mother-line? In your journal, detail the previous four women with whom you are connected womb-to-womb.

    Who were they? Where did they live? Did you know them through stories or personal experience? Do you see threads in the tapestry that lead back to you? Do you look like any of them, do you share any similar traits or experiences? Do you have the same love languages?

- Add something to your altar to represent them. If you own something that has been passed down, add it, or even wear it (such as a piece of jewelry).

- Is it possible to find more stories? Are there questions that need answering? Can you find those answers?

- Remain here or let this ignite a journey into your personal Tree of Life. Do a DNA test to understand your ancestry in more detail. Create a family tree in your journal or as a bigger project.

    Who was she? Who am I? Who are we as a collective?

Connected through Ancient Roots: Creating Intentional Ancestral Reconciliation

- Write a statement of intention to witness your mother-line in its truth, and in turn to see yourself in your truth.

    Honor the stories in your statement, some of which are yours, some theirs, some uplifting, some dark.
    Honor your own journey and stories.
    Honor the roots and the new branches growing.

- Add photographs, drawings, artifacts, or pressed tree leaves to support your statement.

- Find a grandmother tree to meditate and heal with. A grandmother tree is a tree elder, one which supports younger trees through her root system, likened to a human crone in the Pagan tradition. Receive from her love and nurturing. Grow deep roots with her. Give to her a gift of poem, song, crystal, shell, feather, dance, or whatever springs from your heart.

- Journal any transformation, dreams, or insights through this reconciliation.

Ancestor Tarot Spread

- Lay your tarot or oracle cards face down one to seven as you intuitively pull them.

- Turn them over and attune to the cards.

- Ask these questions, or any that you imagine: What is your name and your relationship to me? What life lessons can you help me with? What wisdom do you have for me today? What sign will you use to signal your presence? What gifts have you passed on to me? How can I honor my ancestors more? How can I become a better ancestor?

- Listen for the answers, trust what comes through, write it down, and add to it the meaning or message of the card itself.

- Thank your ancestor for their messages and wisdom.

"The story of all mothers and daughters is the story of their estrangements and their reunions."

— DEMETRA GEORGE

BIRTHING AUTHENTICITY AND YOUR SACRED PATH

By choosing to be responsible for your own joy, you release your mother from being who she could not be.

If your experience has been that you made yourself small in order to be loved, or if you have denied our own authenticity in order to feel safe or accepted, it is your sacred responsibility to love, nurture, and initiate yourself into a life of self-worth.

A woman who feels unsafe, unheard, and unseen, may sacrifice her child in the same way she felt sacrificed. She may ask her, through conscious and unconscious ways, to abandon her truth.

- In which ways did your mother or mother figure extinguish your fire?

- Where in your body do you feel her abandonment?

- In which life situations do you see this denial of Self re-enacted by your own actions or decisions?

  It is common with mother wounds to practice self-aggression and self-wounding when clarity is lacking. To gain clarity, explore the pattern initiated by your mother-line.

- Write an intention to love, nurture, and initiate yourself into your authentic truth and life; to recognize yourself as worthy of expressing all of who you are; and to love and nurture yourself in your uniqueness.

Allow space for your mother to be herself as you would have wanted her to honor your space. Allow space to grieve the Mother you never had, the "real" mother who did not materialize. In letting go of the fantasy mother you expected, you become empowered.

Notice the space that opens in your story when you release the mother you hoped for and accept the experience you had as a path to self-mastery.

Grieving the "real" mother and taking responsibility for our own sacred, authentic path reframes the story and shifts the focus from victim/blame to aligned co-creation.

What would you like to create in your life?

A Ritual for Releasing the Fantasy Mother

- Write a thank-you note to the fantasy mother whom your mother could not live up to.

  Example: *Dear Fantasy Mother, I honor your place in my life, and the ways you kept me in touch with what my needs were. I've kept you close to my heart hoping that you would materialize in my life.*

- Feel all the places where this fantasy mother resides in your body or emotions.

- Place this letter on your altar and honor the feelings that arise when you think of letting her go.

- In a safe container, like a cauldron on your altar, burn this letter with the intention of opening healing space where she once resided.

- Scatter these ashes in a place that feels supportive. A body of moving water is best, or you can scatter the ashes to the wind in your favorite place in nature.

- Create boundaries in your thoughts, speech, and actions that do not invite the fantasy mother to materialize again. Instead fill the space with a journey onto your sacred path and highest embodiment.

*"The true meaning of forgiveness
is not to forget what has happened to you,
but to stop wishing it had been different."*

— TOKO-PA TURNER, *BELONGING*

PART VIII

The Stages of Grief within the Mother Wound

*If we look deep enough,
we can find stories of resilience and
courage within any mother.*

ABANDONMENT
AND GRIEF

We may not realize it, but at the root of the mother wound lies *abandonment*. It is deeply embedded with fear. Our whole process of bonding with life, with ourselves, and finding trust and safety depends on the bond we create with our mother.

No matter when the mother wound is created, during childhood or adulthood (as when mother passes or becomes unstable, slips into Alzheimer's, or suddenly becomes someone we can no longer feel safe around), a cycle of grief becomes our teacher.

The purpose of grief is to soften us, although it may seem the opposite. It, like the Great Mother, moves through seasons.

We may be grieving without consciously putting a label on it. It may feel like depression or sadness; it may be an illness or a complete collapse of the immune system. We may circle it for months or years until it speaks its name. And then one day, aha, grief drops its veil, and we see our manifested relationships and circumstances as our dance with our mother.

Abandonment and grief sometimes show up in:

- Feelings of loss, at times inexplicable or undefined

- Feelings of disappointment in how life has turned out

- Feelings of insecurity or self-doubt, or a lost sense of Self

- A disconnection with one's soul blueprint

- A lingering melancholy in body and spirit

- Fear of the future or of the everyday, and procrastination in "getting on" with life

- Self-sabotage—just when one begins to feel supported by life and the Universe. (This may present itself as unavoidable circumstances that just seem to pop up.)

The Outer Child engages in patterns that mirror the original abandonment of the Inner Child and creates a cycle of self-abandonment.

Recognizing the patterns and clues of grief is step one. Conscious awareness of the stages allows you to hold grief with love and compassion and embrace your journey without judgment.

- **Shock**: Realization of what is happening or has happened (this may surface years after actual trauma)

- **Denial**: Resisting the reality and avoiding the inevitable

- **Anger**: Outpouring of bottled-up emotions or violence/self-destructive behavior from suppressed anger

- **Bargaining**: Seeking for a way out of the situation in vain or the justification of circumstances

- **Depression**: Final sinking into the reality and feeling hopeless. Tasting the pain. Self-wounding.

- **Testing**: Feeling hopeful at times and seeking realistic solutions

- **Acceptance**: Finding the way forward.

- **Compassion and Forgiveness**: Accepting responsibility for your experience and healing, releasing the need to blame, and finding compassion and forgiveness for yourself and your mother

- **Integration into Wholeness**: Reconnection with your soul's blueprint, transformation, and peace in the face of reality

"I have been/am grieving" is a simple yet powerful statement that brings clarity and brings us back to a still point with the mother wound.

It is also important to know that grief may not follow any pattern at all. You may sink and rise, back and forth, through the "stages." Allow yourself space to grieve in your own unique way.

In Mother Wound We Grieve

The mother we did not have or the mother we lost.
   The bonds we did not form.
   The parts of us that weren't loved.
   Our Inner Child's pain.
   Our younger self.
   The conversations we had or did not have.
   The unhealed parts of Self.

The experiences that brought trauma.
The life we did not have, due to initial or self-wounding.
The words we did not hear.
The embraces not received.
Being misunderstood.
Add to this list to express your own personal grief.

CHAKRA CORRESPONDENCES

Grief is experienced through the chakras with color—the chakras are not listed in chronological order here. Notice where the emotion or experience becomes rooted. You can work with this in meditation, digging up the roots of grief. Once dug, envision releasing these roots from your body and sealing the portal.

- Anger: Red, Root Chakra
(Frustration and resentment can become embedded here.)

- Denial: Purple/Indigo, Third Eye
(Refusing to see what is.)

- Bargaining: Blue, Throat
(Self-expression and asking for what we need, often in vain.)

- Depression: Black, 10th Chakra, below our feet
(Earth/grave, tasting the wound.)

- Testing: Yellow/Orange, Sacral/Solar Plexus
(Searching for *realistic* solutions.)

- Acceptance, Compassion, and Forgiveness: Green, Heart Chakra
(A way forward.)

- Integration into Wholeness: White, Crown
(Connection with Self, soul's blueprint, oneness with Great Mother and the Universe.)

Use these stones for altar work, to use in healing rituals, and/or to wear as allies.

- 10th Chakra: black onyx, black tourmaline, obsidian, black pearl, hematite
- Root: agate, bloodstone, garnet, ruby, smoky quartz
- Third Eye: opal, lapis lazuli, sodalite, indigo sapphire
- Throat: aquamarine, turquoise, chalcedony, kyanite, blue lace agate
- Solar Plexus: amber, tiger's eye, citrine, agate, yellow topaz, carnelian
- Heart: jade, emerald, rose quartz, aventurine, carnelian, jasper
- Crown: amethyst, clear quartz, diamond, selenite
- Sacral (Womb): moonstone, carnelian, tourmaline, amber, citrine

BRING IT TO THE ALTAR

Congratulate yourself on the sacred work you have been doing. Take a deep breath and pause. Your commitment to the transformation journey can be celebrated with the following practices. Perhaps it's time to refresh your altar, now that you have met grief through a new lens.

- On the altar of your being
- On your sacred altar
- In your journal
- Through your creativity: art project, song, dance, photos

Witness yourself and your grief process. In witnessing ourselves, we give ourselves permission to feel it all, to understand ourselves better, to become objective, to engage with grief in a healthy way.

- Record the stages of grief you have experienced: which you recognize, which you are in, which you have witnessed and/or healed.

- Create a pouch or bowl of gemstones to support the chakras that need witnessing currently or use color in other ways for the same purpose (clothing, scarves, flowers for the altar, jewelry, candles, etc.).

What is your body and soul calling for now? Choose what resonates from this list or add your own ideas:

- a conversation with your mother

- a self-care ritual, such as a massage, vacation, poem written to yourself, sacred bath, extended period of silence or solitude, or a cord-releasing ritual

- clearer boundaries with your mother, in other relationships, and with your own thoughts and patterns

- a commitment to purpose

- an intention for a way forward, making a clear choice

What ideas did you come up with?

There must be enough safety and love among women and within society for them to grieve their sadness, rage, and losses. Repressed, it gets passed on to the next generation—daughters who become mothers, who birth daughters and sons. Each generation must own their own pain and healing.

PART IX

Releasing Generational Bonds

*Becoming happens when we allow ourselves
to be the very thing that was suppressed
in us by our mothers, society, patriarchy,
and our own fears of loss and abandonment.*

MOTHER WOUNDS ARE
SOUL TRIBE WOUNDS

Your soul tribe consists of anyone who has incarnated to participate in this lifetime's lessons for self-mastery and soul evolution.

They include those you are related to, those with whom you are in romantic relationships (including affairs), your whole family tree, friends, co-workers, seemingly random acquaintances, children lost to death (illness, accident, abortion, miscarriage, violence, etc.), and relatives by law. A soul tribe can number in the thousands.

Did you know that your Inner Child has been/is in relationships with everyone in your soul tribe? She is too young to understand the complexities of your adult life and does not have the tools to process all that you have lived. She is the part of you that remains a child, bearing the gifts of youth, innocence, and naivety from which you can draw daily.

You can help her feel safe, held, heard, and protected. She is an integral part of who you are. Through releasing generational wounds, you offer her a space where she can trust again and feel valued. You offer her the support you may have not received as you developed into womanhood.

Through addressing and releasing generational bonds, you can offer your Inner Child a powerful reset and freedom from the pain-body of those generations. This release will be felt all along the vibrational frequency of many lives. Her and your mother wound are part of this wider wounding. The work you commit to with this ritual may awaken connections; there may be dreams, memories, or unexpected communication from others in your soul tribe. Everything that happens, serves you and your human and spiritual evolution and is neither good nor bad . . . it simply is.

NAMING THE 12 CORE SOUL TRIBE WOUNDS

You will perform this ritual once for all the times you have been incarnated, including all your experiential bonds in this lifetime.

This ritual entails bathing these 12 core wounds with love, compassion, and forgiveness:

- Limiting beliefs

- Violence

- Poverty

- Rage

- Addiction

- Betrayal

- Abandonment

- Loss of culture

- Illness

- Loss of sovereignty

- Suppression of identity

- Degradation of human rights

Step 1. Prepare

Set an intention for your ritual. Keep it simple. Write it down in your journal.

Example: *My intention for this ritual is to release myself from all generational bonds as experienced through my interactions with my present and past soul tribes.*

Take a cleansing bath with any allies you feel drawn to: crystals, candles and altar items beside your bath/shower, essential oils, bath salts, and so on.

Step 2. Create Ritual Space

Choose a place where you feel safe and protected. This may be indoors or outside.

Gather everything you need: your written intention, your written ritual incantation, your journal, a drink to offer the Goddess/Gods you call in (and for you!), what you wish to wear, and any special items you would like to bring into space (drum, rattles, pictures of ancestors, music, a ribbon for cutting bonds, etc.). There is no wrong way to do this. This is your experience to create as you wish. You might want to keep your ritual space very sparse. Listen to your intuition.

Note: If using a ribbon, label one end as "I Am Free," and the other as "All Bonds, Trauma, Disease." If not using a ribbon, you can also visualize the "bond" as a cord leaving your body, roots and all, then sealing the area where you visualized the cord leaving your body with golden light.

Step 3. Open the Ritual

Light candles, incense, or a fire (if you have access to creating one).

Call in the Four Directions and Four Elements and any allies/angels/goddesses/spirit guides whose energy you may want or need. (My staples are Raven, Coyote, Hummingbird, Lilith, Diana, Rowan, Holly, and Oak.) Feel the energy rise as you remain present to all who gather with you.

Invoke protection and clarity by simply asking them to assist you.

Be mindful of any shifts in wind, energy, or emotions. And breathe.

Step 4. Recite the Incantation

Visualize your soul tribe. You do not need to have faces and names or be able to imagine them *all* individually. *The intention is enough.* Picture the energetic cord of light, which is your personal matrix flowing with love and compassion. There is no need to hand karma back between generations or worry about which karma belongs in which place. That no longer matters. We are clearing bonds from pure heart space where there is no separation. This ritual operates with the energy of Unity Consciousness.

Use this as is or as a template for your own wording. Speak your mantra aloud.

Today, I act in sovereignty over my physical, emotional, intellectual, and spiritual bodies with the intention of releasing myself (present, younger, and future self) from all generational bonds created through all lifetimes, and all soul groups with whom I've experienced life on Earth. With a vibration of pure, unconditional love, compassion, and forgiveness, I release myself from all undesired bonds with others, their intentions (known and unknown) toward me, setting us free from all vows, contracts, energetic cords, and disease, releasing to the cosmos across all realities, dimensions, and layers of personal perceptions. I claim back to myself all soul and heart fragments lost to me through all relationships, across every generation, across all time. I send healing to all in my lineage. I release myself from all effects of previous trauma and trauma passed on through the generations. I claim protection over myself and mine and ask that any ancestors who may still be trapped in their own trauma find peace through their angels and guides. Through this I am whole, I am sovereign, and I am free—fully in my power, responsible for all aspects of my Self. As above, so below; as within, so without. And so, it is!

Cut ribbon at this time if using.

Observe how you are feeling in your body, take time to feel and release all tears, emotions, and physical sensations.

Step 5. Close the Ritual

Thank the Four Directions, Four Elements, angels, guides, goddesses, and allies for assisting you in this powerful and permanent shift. Offer a libation to the Goddess who has assisted you. When you feel she has drunk, drink in celebration with Her.

Journal any or all insights, messages, or visions. Meditate, dance, or sing. Blow out your candles when you are ready to return to this realm.

Take the day to rest and connect with the Great Mother. She has witnessed your transformation.

Congratulations!

You have created more peace, love, and unity within yourself, within the world, and within all of Consciousness.

I Am a child of the Universe and the
Great Mother, a spirit having a human experience.
Home is an integral part of me.

SUPPORT FOR YOUR INNER CHILD

An Exercise in Self-Worth

- Read to her, perhaps your favorite childhood stories.

- Surprise her with a gift that will remind her and *you* how special you both are.

- Adventure together. Play is an important aspect of joy.

- Include her in your altar, your prayers, and your daily meditation.

- Play music she may enjoy. Think about what will bring warm, safe memories for you both.

- Share a treat. Sit down at your favorite cafe and indulge in something decadent. No calorie counting—neither of you need permission to do as you please.

- Listen to her. Let her express herself in your journal, your art, and the way you live your life.

- Hold her. She loves warm blankets, cups of hot cocoa, and literal hugs. Make a habit of hugging yourself: breathe out and enjoy the comfort of being held.

- Dream with her. Ask her what she hoped for as she grew. Let her know that her dreams are valid by pursuing any that call to you.

- Teach her about compassion, forgiveness, and living through the heart. She is always listening, watching, and learning. Help her grow strong and confident by making the choices that empower you.

- Love her. Tell her often! She never gets tired of positive affirmation.

Your relationship with your Inner Child is your relationship with the world. It is your sacred responsibility as well as a gift to yourself.

Support your Inner Mother the same way you would support your Inner Child. Witness her with compassion and acceptance. Allow her to grieve, cry, and release. Support her with acts of kindness toward yourself.

Inner Child, Inner Mother, and you are one.

PART X

Shamanic Soul Journey

Sometimes we need to go deeper,
past the psyche,
to the seat of the soul.

IGNITING FORGIVENESS

Meeting Your Inner Child and Mother in a Reconciliation Fire Ritual

In this guided journey, travel to meet yourself at any stage of your life, past, present, or future.

Meet ancestors, spirit guides, animal totems, loved ones (including pets), angels, archetypes, or Interplanetary Beings.

The guided shamanic journey is a safe and sacred container within which you can:

- Speak to your younger or future self.

- Speak to anyone with whom you have unresolved conflicts.

- Remove energetic cords to completed relationships.

- Obtain guidance/wisdom from ancestors or spirit guides.

- Release core wounds from cell memory.

- Clear vows and energetic bonds.

- Facilitate compassion, empathy, emotional healing, and forgiveness.

- Convey messages to loved ones on the Other Side.

- Address mother, father, sibling, or partner wounds.

- Access intuition and your inner Wise One.

The Guided Shamanic Journey allows for alchemical shifts within your soul's evolution.

This ritual is to meet Inner Child and Mother but can also be used to meet with other people/entities in your life, and as such this ritual can be reused many times for different applications.

- Find a comfortable place where you can sit in a meditative state.

- Arrange your surroundings to support the magical experience you are about to enter. Light candles to invite angelic and spirit messengers. Apply essential oils of your choice if you wish to your pulse points. You can use these to bring comfort to you during the journey. Pull a card or two and set them on your altar. Have your journal ready by your side. You will want to record this very important step in your transforming mother wound journey.

- Set an intention for your journey. You can write it down and place on your altar as well.

- Silence and put away your phone.

- Journey in silence or with supportive music.

- Sit now with your body in an alert but comfortable position.

- Take and release three deep breaths. Breathe three breaths of unconditional love and peace. Release all anxiety, fear, and judgment. Breathe in three more breaths of love. Breathe out love, sharing it with the consciousness.

- Close your eyes and begin.

- Find yourself in your body—a safe, warm environment where you feel completely at ease. You will notice a path to follow to your left, and further down the path, a set of stairs that will take you to a deeper part within yourself. Take these steps at a leisurely pace, each one taking you further away from this realm and into a realm where anything is possible. You are no longer in the 3rd Dimension but in the dimension of your heart chakra.

  Your body is filled with light, and you are now a boundless sea of beingness. You are home.

- What is your name in this realm? Answer from your Higher Self. Allow any of your interdimensional names to surface.

  You can begin recording in your journal now, knowing that you remain in the dimension of the heart chakra, even as you write and look around.

- Invite in any of your guides, angels, animal familiars, or a mentor whom you wish to guide you on the journey. What is/are their names?

- Look around and describe what the heart chakra feels like or looks like. What colors do you see? What sensations do you feel here?

  Feel everything fully. Allow raw emotions to surface. Do not edit how you feel. It is safe here to feel. You will be viewing the story of what was but not engaging with the drama of it. Remember, you are not in mind/ego space. You are in heart space.

  In this vast, warm, supportive space, notice how old you are. Write that down. This may be your present self or at any age.

- Ask your mentor/guide or animal familiar (if present) to assist you in lighting a fire and place some seats around it in a sacred circle.

  Pick a memory from your childhood or some other time and invite your younger self and mother to join you in this circle. Ask any other people you wish to also sit at the fire to join you now.

  Take note of where they choose to sit, how old they are, what they are wearing, and anything that seems important to you at this time. You may wish to have your younger self sit near you, so you can hold their hand or offer a hug. Greet your mother with your most honest emotions in this moment.

- Let the memory play out on in your mind's eye, knowing that all those at the fire can also see this memory. You are not reliving it; you are simply observing.

According to the story you let play out on the screen, you can have a conversation with your mother. Ask her anything you need to know and let her answer. Feel your feelings fully as you do this—breathe into it, experience it.

Allow Mother to feel what you are feeling, to see things from your point of view. She will come to understand you in a way she could not have before, or in ways you could not share before.

Remember, you are here as a vast and boundless energy of pure, unconditional love. Record anything your Higher Self may have to say during this experience.

You can step into your mother's heart now to feel what she's feeling as she fully understands your suffering. Allow compassion to wash through you. Through this, you can experience *the best part of your mother, had she known better.* Record what she is feeling as she experiences your previous pain.

Knowing that your mother was probably doing the best she could with the resources she had at the time, what does she have to say about the pain you felt then? *Let her say everything that is on her heart.*

What does your Inner Child/younger self have to say to your mother in response? What does your present self have to say?

Are there any more questions you need to ask your mother? Listen for her answers.

Remember she is speaking from her Higher Self, not the person she was or even is today.

What would have to happen in order for you to reconcile with your mother in this particular memory or in any other memories you wish to clear? After hearing from your mother at soul level, allowing her to feel your pain and witnessing her response, can you conceptualize coming to a degree of, or complete peace with, the situation?

This fire ceremony does not attempt to justify your mother's actions in any way, it simply allows the two of you to meet each other in a safe, nonjudgmental heart space.

- Reassure your younger self as follows:

  "You do not have to experience this pain again. I share with you all the resources I have now to help you deal with anything you may still be struggling with. I love you and will protect, guide, and support you."

- Allow everyone at the fire to dissolve into the ether.

- Now look around the heart space again. How has the region changed around you? What sensations do you feel in your body? In your heart?

- When you are ready, return to the present moment via the same stairs and path you took at the beginning of the ritual. Take your time to notice what the path and stairs look like now and how you are feeling.

- Open your eyes when you are ready.

- While you are fresh from your ritual, write a short (or long) letter to your past self. What advice does she have for your Inner Child?

Your ritual is over. Please nourish your body and drink plenty of water. The days and months to come may reveal new insights. Blessed be.

In a shorter ritual, if you wish to return to more memories or wounds, simply create conversations around the virtual fire with your mother and your younger or present self. Allow them to feel what you are feeling and respond from their Higher Self. Record the conversation and add more layers of reconciliation until those memories no longer contain a charge for you.

FROM CODEPENDENCE TO CO-CREATION

Codependency is common in people who have suffered trauma, abandonment, loss, and abuse.

We can not only be codependent in our physical relationships but also with our thought patterns, resources, and ideas. Certain behaviors, when engaged with, give a type of dopamine effect, and keep us trapped in a cycle of self-abandonment.

Codependence is a loss of Self.

It happens because we become adjusted to thinking that our needs are not important, and that it is safer to tend to the moods, desires, and expectations of those who control our very existence, specifically the mother on whom we rely for appreciation, love, compassion, encouragement, and the guidance to honor our own wisdom.

To become embodied in our purpose, and to be able to function from a place of empowerment, we look honestly at the places in our life where we are more attached to what others think of us, or how we can please, and instead, embrace the knowledge that *we hold all the keys to unlocking our best life.*

When we feel unworthy, we act from shame and guilt.

*"I am not what happened to me.
I am what I choose to become."*

— CARL JUNG

JOURNAL AND ACTION PROMPTS

- In what areas of your life can you listen to your own intuition more and recognize your own authority and sovereignty?

  Take steps to recognize your needs, to acknowledge your own voice, and to give to yourself. There is no one who knows what you need better than yourself.

- You cannot spoil a child with love. Write down 10 ways you can offer affection to yourself. Practice being *Self-ish* from a place of self-worth.

- We recreate our childhoods with behavior that mirrors our mother's detachment. Come back to Self. Write down some patterns you would like to break.

- What is your truth? Create a statement/ mantra that validates your reason for being on Earth and being loved. *"I am here to . . . I deserve to . . . I believe that/in . . . I am a person of . . . [list your qualities and gifts]."*

- In what ways do you give away your power or give away Self? Turn those ways around now. In what ways can you restore your power?

- List your core relationships. What boundaries do you see as being weak in those relationships? Taking responsibility for your boundaries, without apologizing for doing so (you have every right to protect yourself), implement changes and watch yourself leap into deeper embodiment of purpose!

- When we crave the mother we did not have, we seek substitutions in other relationships. Write down one to three things you will no longer tolerate in your life, including self-sabotaging habits.

- Our relationship with abundance/resources/money is reflected in our relationship with ourselves. Thoughts such as "I don't need much," "I never have enough," and "It's not important to me," or in reverse, hoarding money and not giving ourselves what we need are ways we enact shame around abundance. The core statements that we have absorbed are "I am not enough. I do not deserve. There is not enough for ME."

  Try this mantra or one you create yourself to initiate a healthy relationship with abundance. Commit it to paper and/or speak out loud.

  Mantra: *I am enough. I am abundant. I create my own resources from within. My desires are supported by the Universe.*

- Independence does not mean that we do not care for others. It means that we do not become enmeshed in their lives so far as to block their ability to *care for themselves*. Living for Self is a recognition of our own worth. A balance of these is making sure that we have a full cup before we pour for someone else. No one can sustainably live their purpose from a place of self-deprivation.

Journal ways in which you are stepping into your sovereignty, and allowing others theirs.

Mantra: *I respect my authority over my own life. I am self-reliant, and I love who I have become and am becoming. I give from a full well of abundance.*

- It is perfectly okay to be a giver, to be generous, as long as it is not from a place of fear or guilt. You are responsible for yourself now. You will not be abandoned if you do not give or please enough because you practice healthy boundaries with yourself and others. You will not be rejected or be expected to be perfect.

  List one way in which you have become a co-creator in your life, and have released fear, trusting that you will be safe in your decisions.

- Connectedness is what every human being craves in order to self-actualize. When we face the fear of those dark places within ourselves, and when we embrace fear born of being rejected, abused, abandoned, or neglected, we find that *it can dissipate simply by being felt instead of being avoided*! We get through it. We see that it has an end. Then, we can connect deeply to ourselves, to Spirit, to the Great Mother, and to others without losing Self.

In what ways do you feel stronger now that you have faced the dark shadows of your mother wound? Celebrate your courage and the work you have done.

EXCERPT FROM
THE MOTHERHOOD CONSPIRACY

by Galina Singer

So much of modern parents' efforts are spent on providing material well-being, but not on the emotional and spiritual bonding with each other or their children. Often, it is that pressure of chasing perfection and material expansion—projecting our own unrealized ambitions and fears of scarcity and survival on our children—that promotes and creates the split between us and our children.

Our children do not need more toys or a bigger bedroom. They need more interaction and the ability to explore new things without attachment to outcome or *performance*. If we are always focused on the goals and trying to get our children to a certain milestone, we are missing out on what is going on with them or who they are right now. When they are not accepted for who they are, our children will go on to demand certain behaviors from their relationships, rather than accepting people for who they are. Our children do not care how young or thin we are. And yet it is our own inner struggles that prevent us from properly bonding with our children, or anyone else in our lives.

It is our own capacity to meet ourselves in compassion and unconditional love that can provide an accepting and loving environment for our children. As cruel and non-accepting as we are to ourselves is how we show up for all our relationships.

The mother preoccupied with her internal suffering is lost to the child. The children sense that their mother is elsewhere and take it personally. They then carry the grief of the loss of their mother to her sadness, to her internal preoccupations, to her anger, to her sense that her life has been stolen from her.

Motherhood is a choice that creates consequences that ripple out way beyond our own lives.

Galina Singer, author and unconventional
relationship coach

*One way to heal the past and future
is to be here now.*

PART XI

Loving Self

The Feminine Mystery

*We can be living in the now and
healing core wounds from the past.
In fact, rooted in presence is the safest
way to address our story.*

BEAUTIFUL
EMBODIED YOU

Journal ways in which you have grown into self-love through exploring your mother wound.

- What do you think has been a pivotal moment in your quest to uncover mother-wound shadows?

- Where did you feel a shift in how you view yourself against the background of your story?

- Add to your altar something that signifies how you feel about yourself today, having done all this work.

HONORING EMOTION
AND CHAOS

The Divine Feminine represents the right brain, emotion, chaos, and intuition; receiving, nurturing, surrendering to love, and healing; and being gentle, wise, expressive, patient, flexible, creative, soft, peaceful, heart-centered, flowing, expansive, and inner focused.

- Which of these qualities do you feel safe expressing and being? Which describe who you are already?

- Do you see the qualities you noted as valuable, or have they in the past been a source of vulnerability?

- Is there room in your relationship with your mother to express yourself as chaos and emotion?

  Does it feel safe, or do you have a role to play?
  What is this role?
  Can you give yourself permission to step out of your role and into your full embodiment?

- How real can you be with your mother? Are you allowed to express your wildness without apology?

- What parts of you do you wish you could be real about with your mother?

- What qualities are you withholding from yourself? Is there anything you wish to say to yourself, about who you are at your core, and give yourself permission to be?

  The Divine Masculine represents the left brain, logic, adventure, action, reason, strength, and survival; being firm, loyal, rational, aggressive, mind-centered, and assertive, analytical; as well as being emotionally guarded, outer focused, and a planner.

- Which of these qualities do you see in yourself?

- How can you bring more balance to your inherent feminine/masculine essence?

- We are culturally conditioned to express what is thought to be gender correct, and to suppress what is thought to be incorrect. Have you been asked to be more of one than the other? Perhaps shamed into "right" behavior? How?

- In which areas of your life do you feel you need more balance? What requires more of your masculine or more of your feminine?

- Balanced, do you feel more courage to assert and claim your full embodiment on Earth?

- If you were to write a letter to your mother, what would you tell her about the masks you wish to take off, or which roles you will no longer play to please her or your Inner Child. This is standing in your power, because the only validation you can be sure of being granted is the one you give yourself.

I will no longer wear the mask of . . .
I Am . . .

HONORING PASSION AND DESIRE

Lover. Priestess of Sensuality. Creatress of Life.

Your sexuality is the life force of the Universe through which all is created. It is a sacred flow of the Divine through you. It powers everything you create in your life.

Your yoni and womb are the sacred cauldrons in which all life is begun. It is a mystery how spirit and body are knit together, deep within a woman's body, and how desire and sexuality are the conduits for human incarnation. Desire is the seed of all life.

Mantras for Life

- *My sexuality is sacred.*
- *I am free to express my desire and sexuality.*
- *I adore my yoni and offer her rituals of love.*
- *I deserve deep pleasure.*
- *Life is pleasure.*
- *I am pleasure.*
- *I am turned on by life.*
- *I honor my personal sexual preferences and explore them with freedom.*
- *I take pleasure in life.*
- *Desire is my birthright.*

- *I love my body, and thank it for its service.*
- *I am naked in my emotions.*
- *My heart and yoni are connected through love and compassion.*
- *My sexuality is ecstatic.*
- *I explore my sexuality and feel empowered by my choices.*
- *My breasts, yoni, and womb are part of my sovereignty and are respected and held holy.*
- *I am irreverent.*
- *I am a sexual being.*
- *My sexual energy flows through all my chakras.*
- *Pleasure and desire are sacred.*
- *My yoni represents the Great Mother and the Divine Feminine.*

Use the yoni mudra during meditation to calm the nervous system and embrace clam and peace.

Your yoni is your energetic heart!

- Practice yoni gazing. In worshiping the yoni, appreciating her beauty and presence, we remember our own divinity and that pleasure is our birthright.

- Consider using a yoni egg to connect with your sacred sexuality, strengthen your pelvic floor, and deepen your sexual practice and your emotions around sensuality.

- Create a sensuality practice. You are your own best lover, most connected with your desire, needs, and kinks. Practicing self-love reminds the body that she is loved, respected, and appreciated. It *reclaims* your body for yourself.

- Embrace the wild woman within who is free of shame and condemnation for her raw impulses.

- Take a picture of your beautiful yoni. Consider adding it to your altar or journal.

- Write what you love or don't love about your yoni, body, and sexuality. Offer a prayer to your body and sexuality forgiving yourself for any ways you may have ignored, shamed, or abused them. Offer loving-kindness to yourself for the journey you have been on, and in the knowing that you did the best you could with the understanding you had at the time.

*"Talk to yourself the way you'd talk
to someone you love."*

— BRENÉ BROWN

PART XII

Crossing the Threshold

*Our joy and our sorrow can
coexist peacefully within us.*

WELCOME TO YOUR EMERGENCE

Through the process of intentionally delving into the mother wound for the purpose of transmutation, we can symbolically re-enter the womb and rebirth ourselves as women aligned to purpose.

This is accomplished through *Intention*, the magic used by all mystics to create and manifest desired outcomes.

Our soul's greatest desire is to actualize to *purpose*.

When we find transformation through understanding our mother, accepting her role in our life along with her gifts and limitations, and when we find compassion and forgiveness for her, *we find those same things for ourselves* and open to stepping into our purpose and power.

All along, this has been the alchemical soul-shift occurring as we heal the mother wound through Divine Feminine wisdom.

To step into purpose is to come into embodiment as a spiritual being having a human experience.

Write Your Intention

- In your journal, write an intention for stepping into your purpose and power. This can be one sentence or many.

    Example: *My desire is to discover the parts of myself that reveal my soul purpose, and with clear intention step into my empowerment by loving myself as I am, while seeking divine growth.*

Let whatever wants to come flow, in your own words—they will be perfect as they are. Feel this intention. This invites Source to co-create with you.

Create a Vision Board

Whether physical or virtual (on Pinterest, etc.) a vision board is a powerful representation of what you *feel* your purpose is or may be (knowing that your soul-purpose evolves as you do).

On my board, I have things that excite my soul, such as images of books, gardens, beautiful interior design, architecture, chickens, anything that helps me connect with what is sacred to me. The images speak of a simple life, sacred geometry, silence, wisdom. This unfolded into my purpose of being an Earth-keeper and mentor, but more importantly, being of service, which is my true purpose, no matter how I express it, professionally or personally.

Purpose is not what we do; it is who we are.

Embrace a New Vision

- Take a photo of yourself (or have someone help you) in the woods, by a stream, in a field, or anywhere in nature that speaks to you. Dress according to your current desire to express Self. You can be clothed or sky-clad. Close to the Great Mother, embraced by her eternal love and grace, envision the woman who has emerged through her mother-wound journey.

- Add to this photo a revised version of your mother wound story.

  From which new perspective can you write your story?
  How has your perspective shifted?
  Often, my clients say that the story is vastly different from the one they wrote before. It is less about the things that happened—less itemized or full of rehashed memories—and more a story of transformation and wisdom for themselves and others.

- What pieces of you have been retrieved during this journey?

  Example: *Confidence, wisdom, self-trust, self-love, self-empowerment, voice*
  Add these insights to your story.

- Journal about where abundance has already appeared in the months since you began your journey, and what you would like to manifest in the future from your new state of awareness.

Abundance flows in the space created by stepping into compassion and forgiveness. Feel into the places where you have released and made room for new blessings.

"*Every decision I make is a choice between a grievance and a miracle. I choose the miracle. When you make a choice, you change the future.*"

— DEEPAK CHOPRA

REBIRTHING INTO ALIGNED PURPOSE

"Your birth was your first act of courage."

— KATE CALLAHAN

To be born-again is to be present to Self, to understand ourselves in the context of the events that have shaped us but do not define us.

It is to release all victimhood and embrace empowerment by creating the life we wish.

Life does not happen to us. We create it with our thoughts, words, and actions.

- To start this exercise, gather the following items: a long stick (it can be a broomstick, branch, or a piece sturdy string); a bowl of salt, sage, or palo santo; candles; and a journal.

- Cast a circle of salt into which you and the stick will fit easily. If you do not wish to use salt, you can cast an imaginary circle using your broom, athame, or finger!

- Arrange candles, crystals, and any sacred objects you wish around the circle.

- Find music that inspires you into joy.

- Prepare by meditating and setting an intention in your journal for rebirthing into your intended purpose, health, empowerment, ease of being, and soul's blueprint free of previous challenges presented by the mother wound.

- Light candles. (Be careful with fire around your clothes as you step into the circle!)

- Invite all allies, ancestors, spirit guides, elements, goddesses, et cetera, whom you wish to accompany you in your rebirthing.

- Record in your journal any emotions that surface.

- Step into the circle, stand on one side of the stick, and connect with all energies present. Take your time. There is no hurry.

- When centered, grounded, and ready, say these words as you step over the stick:

  I am reborn.
  I am embodied.
  I am on purpose.
  I am whole.
  I Am.

Congratulations, Wild Woman, you have birthed yourself with clear intention, empowered and responsible for your own emergence! Your life will continue to shift, focus, and stretch you. Perhaps you wish to dance, sing, or howl!

Thank all guides and elements present for supporting you in this ritual. With your hands at your heart center, step out of the circle and emerge as Wild, Free, and Embodied as you were meant to be at your birth. Record all of it in your journal.

"*The psyches and souls of women also have*
their own cycles and seasons of doing and solitude,
running and staying, being involved and being removed,
questing and resting, creating and incubating, being of
the world and returning to the soul-place."

— CLARISSA PINKOLA ESTÉS

CLOSING PRAYER

Great Mother,

Thank you for the gifts of birth and rebirth.

For your healing touch, your embrace, your guidance.

Thank you for the gifts of your womb—

the knowing that I am Creatress,

Alchemist, and birther of my own reality.

May I remember the wisdom of my mother-line,

*and take the medicine of my experiences to create
transformation for myself and others.*

When we heal, we become the healer.

Teach me which lessons to pass on

and which to let fall away.

My voice carries the song of my ancestors,

the women who came before me.

May my voice ring true for the generations ahead of me.

May my song echo the ancient stories of all womankind.

*May my heart be filled with love and compassion for all
mothers, including myself.*

May we all rise, hand in hand,

stronger for the journey of our lifetimes.

We rise in gratitude.

And so, it is.

MOVING FORWARD WITH PACHAMAMA

A Magical Shamanic Practice

Flowers, trees, weeds, roots, and fruits contain healing codes, which over the centuries have been discovered and applied by wise women, shamans, and practitioners of natural healing.

Essential oils are powerful allies that can be engaged with during meditation, in a grounding/centering practice, or to release stuck emotions.

Wearing the "spirit" of the plant is a way of communicating directly with the Great Mother. It is a way of energetically being comforted by Her and experiencing her love.

Use only the highest-quality oils, not only for the best healing potential, but also to honor the plants in the way they are grown, harvested, and prepared.

Important note: Sustainability in essential oil production is paramount.

Magical Practice

Choose 1 to 12 plant essences to work with for the next year. To commit one year to a magical practice is to commit yourself to a year of intentional creativity and manifestation. It will affect other areas of your life, including a deeper awareness of purpose and soul evolution.

Add to your mother wound journal or a separate one (this can be an online journal), the following:

- The name and image of the plant (including its Latin name)

- Its spiritual association and healing gift (what it is used for)

- Any history you wish to explore (example: rose has a very ancient applications and meanings)

- What it means to you and how your relationship with this plant spirit has developed

- Any magical synchronicities or healing due to your work with this plant

- How do you feel when you smell the aroma? What emotions come up?

Begin and end your communication and connection work with each plant with an expression of gratitude.

An alternative is becoming a Tree Mother and working with 12 trees instead of oils.

*I am safe to be in my fullness and take up all the space
I need in the world. I am safe to pursue the path I
envisioned, desired, and trained for before I incarnated.
The whole of the Universe, my guides, and my ancestors
support me on my journey. I embody my purpose.*

DARK TEACHER

by Jesica Nodarse

Shadow work is a practice
It's a devotion
A system of self-assessment
It's not just tears and dark nights
It not just calls upon Hekate and Lilith
It is so much more than entropy and pain
It is that extra filter we installed so we can check into our
empathy before judging
It's the insights into your painful childhood that hit you
while doing dishes
The extra breath you take while stuck in traffic
to find your center
I do not discourage your wails
The altars you're called to create
The way Kali or Yemayá burns in your blood
I welcome it all
But it's so much more
It's devotion to our truth
Remembrance of who came before us
It's finding your humble
It's holding the child you were
Honoring the teen within who fought to be heard
And making space for the lessons as well as the pain felt
It's the light within that shines
And the darkness that heals
It's a promise to oneself that says
"I will not be ignorant of my own ways"
It is awareness

Jesica Nodarse, artist

About the Author

Monika Carless is a globally published author and mentor to Earthkeepers, Witches, and Creatives. She lives a quiet life on Vancouver Island focused on simple pleasures with her partner of many moons. Her heart song is guiding women to their sovereignty and fearless authenticity. Especially interested in archetypes, myths, and life mastery through self-healing practices, Monika mines wisdom from her crone years and the healing powers of art and words.

Daily Wise Woman inspiration can be found on Instagram: **@monikacarless**.

Her books include The Dark Pool Trilogy and *Tessa and the Faeries*.

To work with Monika, connect via **monikacarless.com**.

Contributors

Many thanks to the following authors for their contribution to this course book. Please take a moment to check out more of their work via the links below.

Sarah Norrad: sarahnorrad.com
Galina Singer: galinasinger.com
Sophie Gregoire: sophiegregoire.com
Tanya Markul: tanyamarkul.com
Jesica Nodarse: facebook.com/heathenwordsmith

Hay House Titles of Related Interest

YOU CAN HEAL YOUR LIFE, the movie,
starring Louise Hay & Friends
(available as an online streaming video)
www.hayhouse.com/louise-movie

THE SHIFT, the movie,
starring Dr. Wayne W. Dyer
(available as an online streaming video)
www.hayhouse.com/the-shift-movie

***

AWAKENING YOUR INNER SHAMAN: A Woman Hero's Quest,
by Marcela Lobos

*MOTHER HUNGER: How Adult Daughters Can Understand and
Heal from Lost Nurturance, Protection, and Guidance,*
by Kelly McDaniel

TRAUMA: Healing Your Past to Find Freedom Now,
by Pedram Shojai, O.M.D, and Nick Polizzi

*YOU ARE THE MEDICINE: 13 Moons of Indigenous Wisdom,
Ancestral Connection, and Animal Spirit Guidance,*
by Asha Frost

All of the above are available at www.hayhouse.co.uk.

***

MEDITATE.
VISUALIZE.
LEARN.

Get the **Empower You**
Unlimited Audio *Mobile App*

Get unlimited access to the entire Hay House audio library!

You'll get:

- 500+ inspiring and life-changing **audiobooks**
- 700+ ad-free **guided meditations** for sleep, healing, relaxation, spiritual connection, and more
- Hundreds of audios **under 20 minutes** to easily fit into your day
- **Exclusive content** *only* for subscribers
- No credits, **no limits**

New audios added every week!

 ★★★★★ **I ADORE** this app.
I use it almost every day. Such a blessing. – Aya Lucy Rose

Scan me with
your phone camera!

TRY FOR FREE!
Go to: hayhouse.co.uk/audio

CONNECT WITH
HAY HOUSE
ONLINE

🌐 hayhouse.co.uk   **f** @hayhouse

📷 @hayhouseuk   𝕏 @hayhouseuk

▶ @hayhouseuk   ♪ @hayhouseuk

Find out all about our latest books & card decks • Be the first to know about exclusive discounts • Interact with our authors in live broadcasts • Celebrate the cycle of the seasons with us • Watch free videos from your favourite authors • Connect with like-minded souls

'*The gateways to wisdom and knowledge are always open.*'

Louise Hay